D1720561

Michael Negri

Motivation and Punishment of Referees in non-professional Football

An Analysis of existing Problems and the Development of Solution Strategies with particular Regard to the Principal-Agent Theory

Diplomica® Verlag GmbH

Negri, Michael: Motivation and Punishment of Referees in non-professional Football. An Analysis of existing Problems and the Development of Solution Strategies with particular Regard to the Principal-Agent Theory, Hamburg, Diplomica Verlag GmbH 2010

ISBN: 978-3-8428-5224-2
Druck: Diplomica® Verlag GmbH, Hamburg, 2010

Bibliografische Information der Deutschen Nationalbibliothek:
Die Deutsche Nationalbibliothek verzeichnet diese Publikation in der Deutschen Nationalbibliografie; detaillierte bibliografische Daten sind im Internet über http://dnb.d-nb.de abrufbar.

Die digitale Ausgabe (eBook-Ausgabe) dieses Titels trägt die ISBN 978-3-8428-0224-7 und kann über den Handel oder den Verlag bezogen werden.

Dieses Werk ist urheberrechtlich geschützt. Die dadurch begründeten Rechte, insbesondere die der Übersetzung, des Nachdrucks, des Vortrags, der Entnahme von Abbildungen und Tabellen, der Funksendung, der Mikroverfilmung oder der Vervielfältigung auf anderen Wegen und der Speicherung in Datenverarbeitungsanlagen, bleiben, auch bei nur auszugsweiser Verwertung, vorbehalten. Eine Vervielfältigung dieses Werkes oder von Teilen dieses Werkes ist auch im Einzelfall nur in den Grenzen der gesetzlichen Bestimmungen des Urheberrechtsgesetzes der Bundesrepublik Deutschland in der jeweils geltenden Fassung zulässig. Sie ist grundsätzlich vergütungspflichtig. Zuwiderhandlungen unterliegen den Strafbestimmungen des Urheberrechtes.

Die Wiedergabe von Gebrauchsnamen, Handelsnamen, Warenbezeichnungen usw. in diesem Werk berechtigt auch ohne besondere Kennzeichnung nicht zu der Annahme, dass solche Namen im Sinne der Warenzeichen- und Markenschutz-Gesetzgebung als frei zu betrachten wären und daher von jedermann benutzt werden dürften.

Die Informationen in diesem Werk wurden mit Sorgfalt erarbeitet. Dennoch können Fehler nicht vollständig ausgeschlossen werden, und der Diplomica Verlag, die Autoren oder Übersetzer übernehmen keine juristische Verantwortung oder irgendeine Haftung für evtl. verbliebene fehlerhafte Angaben und deren Folgen.

© Diplomica Verlag GmbH
http://www.diplomica-verlag.de, Hamburg 2010
Printed in Germany

Table of Contents

1 Introduction

"Contradicting the referee is like standing up in the church to ask for a discussion."[1] This admittedly exaggerated appreciation of a football referee nonetheless shows that a neutral institution in football matches seems to be essential. Especially in professional football, referees play an important role as they are the "judges" in a game that has developed into an entertainment industry in the past years. However, not only the professional football needs referees. In comparison to the 10,000 professional football players, about 6,500,000 amateurs actively play this sport. This, in return, means that there are far more referees in non-professional football.

The focus of this work is to examine how effective punishments and motivational means can be in order to improve the interaction between the players in a Principal-Agent constellation. The analyzed case deals with referees in non-professional football (Agents) and their interaction with the supervising managing-committee (Principal)[2] in the district of Guetersloh, Germany. As the committee is responsible for the referee training, development and assignment, the persons in charge do have a basic interest in motivated referees. However, the reason for the unsatisfactory situation seems to result from exactly those mentioned motivational issues. The insufficient participation in the monthly meetings, the absence during the yearly examination and the lack of willingness to take over matches are only a few of the current problems, the managing-committee is confronted with.

The question which shall be answered in the course of this work will be: **How can the problems in the work of the referee managing-committee be solved with particular regard to the PAT ('Principal-Agent Theory'), motivation and punishment?**

---

[1] „Dem Schiedsrichter zu widersprechen, das ist, wie wenn man in der Kirche aufsteht und eine Diskussion verlangt" (Original quotation by Dieter Hildebrandt, a German cabaret artist, actor and author)
[2] For simplicity reasons, expressions that may comprise male and female persons will be considered as male in the further course of the work. Of course, all of them can just as well be female

In order to answer this question with a special focus on the effectiveness of motivation, the Principal-Agent Theory will be applied as theoretical basis and shall be backed up by elements of Maslow's Hierarchy of Needs and Vroom's Expectancy Theory. The role of punishment shall be analyzed with the help of the Deterrence Hypothesis. As this case is also relevant for the work of managing-committees in other districts and countries, practical recommendations for improvement will be developed without neglecting the given constraints in this issue.

This work is split up into eight sections. Following the introduction, section two will introduce the basic issues of this work, directly leading to the explanation of the author's motivation for the given topic and the relevance for other parties involved. Furthermore, the scientific approach of this analysis will be explained. The third section will introduce the key terms in the context of this work whereas the following section will set the theoretical framework. Section five focuses on the presentation of the case. This includes the explanation of the referees` organizational framework, but also the display of the prevalent problems in the case. Moreover, the case solution (Section 6) aims at applying the theories and the empirical survey to the problems in order to find practical solution mechanisms. Section seven critically evaluates the applied theories and the empirical survey that was conducted in regard to their contribution to the case solution. Finally, the work ends with a conclusion and an outlook.

The main findings in regard to motivational issues and the role of punishment were derived from the empirical survey. Additionally, the application of the Principal-Agent Theory delivers further solutions. As the activity is a hobby, the referees in non-professional football do not feel that they have to be committed extraordinarily, but rather expect appreciation of their dedication. This attitude is the basic trigger of the problems described. In order to solve those, a positive enforcement of the referees` behavior seems to be more promising than to punish misbehavior. Especially appealing to the morale and the introduction of a formal 'contract' represent promising approaches. However, in the long run, the number of referees has to be significantly increased in order to let the referees` performance and behavior become decisive factors again. This can be reached by increasing the PR ('Public Relations') efforts and by improving the recruitment process.

2 Problem and Methodology

The section shall introduce the basic problems that are analyzed in this thesis. It also examines the reason for choosing this particular topic and illustrates the importance for the persons in charge of organizing the functioning referee system. Furthermore, the scientific methodology will be introduced in order to illustrate the setup of this work.

2.1 Problem Definition and Relevance

The managing-committee in the district of Guetersloh has experienced various problems in the work with referees. Despite the fact that the number of referees only hardly suffices to assign an arbitrator to every match each weekend, the active referees do not seem to be adequately motivated. This impression results from their missing willingness to attend the monthly meetings and the annual examination. Both are important appointments for each referee, because they serve as a means of theoretical and practical development. Furthermore, many referees cancel their assignment to a match very shortly before the beginning of the actual match. In consequence, the person in charge of the referee assignments has to reshuffle the assignments already conducted. Another severe problem is the referees` tendency to be more and more open to fraud. This means that especially close to the end of a season, representatives of clubs approach the referees in order to bribe them. It shall be examined within this work, how frequently clubs try to influence referees and their decisions by offering incentives, and what exactly these bribes consist of.

The managing-committee is well aware of all these issues. However, it seems as if there are no effective means to solve these problems. Frey (2009) describes how such a measure can look like. According to him, applying punishment has been used as a dominant tool to deter people from committing crimes in the last decades.[3] Although fines are applied in the referees` case, they do not have the desired effect of enforcing compliance. For example, there are administrative fines for referees who are absent without excuse on a monthly meeting.

---

[3] Cf. Frey (2009, p. 1)

However, these fines are paid by the clubs where the respective referee is a member, making them very ineffective. Due to the fact that there is already a lack of referees, the managing-committee can hardly discard any referee as a form of punishment. As can be seen, the current forms of punishments do not have the desired deterrent effect and leave room for improvement. Keser and Willinger (2002) argue that another way to approach problems that result from a constellation in which one person acts on behalf of another is to motivate him or her by incentives.[4] Nonetheless, the managing-committee has not yet managed to install appropriate incentives to increase motivation among the referees.

This work shall therefore analyze the role of punishment in regard to the referees` behavior. It shall also be elaborated, under which circumstances they can be more effective without neglecting the costs of enforcement.[5] Furthermore, it will be examined which factors influence the motivation of the arbitrators. With these findings, practical recommendations will be made to improve the relationship between the referees and their managing-committee. The previously described problems are not only valid for the district of Guetersloh. As the managing-committee stands in close contact with other districts, it has become obvious that the situation is seemingly similar there as well. The neighboring districts also have an interest in elaborating on the motives of referees in non-professional football accordingly. The findings then shall be applied to the work in the committee in order to improve the current status quo. Furthermore, the author´s role as a member of the managing-committee in the district of Guetersloh has strengthened the interest to find a practical approach to the issues mentioned. In the recent past, the development of this honorary commitment has worsened and demands for countermeasures.

There has been much work done on motivational topics in professional sports. However, the non-professional segment has rather been neglected in this regard. Especially football referees have not been in the focus of research interests, although studying the motives of 78,617 referees in Germany seems to allow for promising findings.[6]

---

[4] Cf. Keser/Willinger (2002, p. 2)
[5] Cf. Miceli (2004, p. 290)
[6] See http://www.dfb.de for more details on the referees in Germany. Information on referees is only available in German.

Basing on these reasons, the analysis of the described issues can contribute interesting findings to the topic of motivation and the effectiveness of referees in non-professional football.

2.2 Research Methods

In order to elaborate valid findings, this work comprises both primary and secondary literature and data. On the one hand, the literature on the Principal-Agent Theory will be examined. On the other hand, the scientific findings on the deterrent effect of punishment, but also motivation will be included. The interaction between the managing-committee and the referees can be displayed as a form of Principal-Agent relationship because the committee assigns the referees to act as a neutral arbitrator in football matches.[7] Although there does not exist an explicit contract between these parties, the managing-committee still is interested in a well-functioning referee system. However, the committee cannot directly influence the referees` performance during the matches. Besides this view on incomplete contracts and asymmetric information in firms, motivational aspects and punishment shall help to reduce the problems resulting from this constellation. Abraham Maslow`s[8] Needs Hierarchy and Vroom`s Expectancy Theory[9] shall be consulted to elaborate on further motivational issues. In order to learn more about incentive structures, the related paper "Intrinsic and Extrinsic Motivation"[10] by Roland Bénabou[11] and Jean Tirole[12] (2003) can be taken into consideration. In their work, the authors study the conditions under which extrinsic incentives can be powerful and counterproductive.

---

[7] Cf. Anderhub/Gaechter/Koenigstein (2002, p. 2)

[8] Abraham Harold Maslow (* 1 April, 1908 in Brooklyn, New York; † 8 June, 1970 in California) was an American psychologist. He is well-known for his conceptualization of the "hierarchy of human needs", and is considered the founder of humanistic psychology

[9] Victor Vroom (*9 August, 1932 in Montreal, Canada) is a business school professor at the Yale School of Management. The focus of his scientific research is set on work, motivation, and leadership

[10] Bénabou/Tirole (2003)

[11] Roland Bénabou is Professor of Economics and Public Affairs at Princeton University

[12] Jean Tirole (*1953) is a French professor of economics and Director of the Industrial Economics Institute in Toulouse. His scientific focus is on game theory, industrial organization, banking and finance, and economics and psychology

Bruno S. Frey[13] and Reto Jegen[14] (2000) analyze how extrinsic incentives and punishment impact the intrinsic motivation of people under certain circumstances in their paper "Motivation Crowding Theory: A Survey or Empirical Evidence."[15]

In addition to the secondary literature, a questionnaire was set up to support the findings from the relevant literature. Its intention is to elaborate on the basic motivational aspects of referees in the district of Guetersloh. Furthermore, the questionnaire shall help to learn more about the effectiveness of punishment. The recommendations drawn from the theories then shall be compared with the results from the questionnaires in order to evaluate how relevant the theories really are. In the end, realizable measures shall be presented.

3 Key Terms: Punishment and Motivation

In the further course of the thesis, various notions and key terms will be of central importance. The definitions do not claim to be universally and overall valid, but rather shall create a concrete understanding of the respective term used for this work. In the following, the central understanding of 'Motivation' and 'Punishment' for this thesis will be introduced.

3.1 Motivation

In this thesis, the notion 'Motivation' will be understood as a process of encouraging people to act in a way that leads to a certain aim.[16] According to Wong (2000), motivation additionally has to do with the reasons for performing a specific action.[17] In accordance with Mook (1987) it means understanding why people do certain things and show determination in certain situations.[18] In the case context, motivation is therefore the referees´ determination to comply with the existing regulations. Moreover, motivating people at the same time means to 'manipulate' them by appealing to their needs.

---

[13] Bruno S. Frey is Professor of economics at the Institute for Empirical Economic Research, University of Zurich
[14] Reto Jegen is research assistant at the Institute for Empirical Economic Research, University of Zurich
[15] Frey/Jegen (2000)
[16] Cf. Scott/R. Mitchell (1972, p. 76)
[17] Cf. Wong (2000, p. 3)
[18] Cf. Mook (1987, p. 4)

The existing literature also distinguishes between intrinsic and extrinsic motivation.[19] Intrinsic motivation is considered to be based on an individual`s wish for self-determination and empowerment.[20] Intrinsically motivated people do not expect any form of external reward when performing a certain task. According to O`Neil/Drillings (1994), they rather act for their own sake and see the task itself as a form of reward.[21] Besides intrinsic reasons, motivation can also be enforced by external determinants such as salary, obligations, fines or grades in school.[22] These means can be applied as a reward for positive behavior, but also as a punishment for misdemeanor.[23]

3.2 Punishment

Punishing misbehavior generally can be an effective means to foster compliance of individuals. In order to create a common understanding of what is considered as 'punishment', the following definition will be assumed. Thus, "[…] punishment is viewed as the presentation to a person as something aversive or the removal of something pleasant."[24] It includes mild actions, such as reprimand, but also severe ones, which can be for example arrest. According to Golash (2005), punishment basically is the infliction of negative consequences as a consequence for doing something wrong.[25]

4 Theoretical Background

This part of the thesis will introduce and explain the theories which are relevant for the case. As a first step, the Principal-Agent Theory will be illustrated. In the following, Becker`s Deterrence Hypothesis will be explained. Finally, Maslow`s Needs Hierarchy and Vroom`s Expectancy Theory will be introduced.

---

[19] Cf. Deci/Ryan (2000, pp. 227-268)
[20] Cf. Miner (2005, p. 109)
[21] Cf. O`Neil/Michael Drillings (1994, p. 83)
[22] Cf. Coon/Mitterer (2008, p. 339)
[23] Cf. Weinberg/Gould (2007, p. 139)
[24] Huesmann/ Podolski (2003, p. 59)
[25] Cf. Golash (2005, p. 1)

4.1 The Principal-Agent Theory

The Principal-Agent Theory has been discussed thoroughly in recent years and allows for a systematic approach to problems resulting from incomplete contracts and asymmetric information whenever someone acts on behalf of another person.[26] According to Williamson (1985), the more specific an investment is, the more incomplete the underlying contract is.[27] Generally, the theory examines the interaction and behavior of a principal, in this case represented by the managing committee, the so called KSA ('Kreis-Schiedsrichterausschuss'),[28] and the agent (the referees). The theory has its roots in the findings by Ronald H. Coase[29] who has made a huge contribution to the question why firms exist at all with his works "The Nature of the Firm" (1937) and "The Problem of Social Cost" (1960). In the former, Coase points out that a firm is a network of incomplete contracts which are intended to formalize the interaction between various parties involved.[30]

Following Coase` findings, Oliver E. Williamson[31] coined the notion of "New Institutional Economics"[32] which comprises the Property Rights Theory[33], the Transaction Cost Theory[34], the Contract Theory,[35] and the Principal-Agent Theory.[36] According to Pratt and Zeckhauser (1985), a Principal-Agent relationship occurs when a person depends on the performance of another. In this case, the former is called the principal, the latter is the agent.[37]

---

[26] Cf. Chambers/Quiggin (2003, p. 1)
[27] Cf. Willamson (1985)
[28] The "Kreis-Schiedsrichterausschuss" is the managing committee of the referees in Guetersloh. It consists of seven permanent members. The KSA is chaired by KSO ('Kreis-Schiedsrichterobmann'). He leads a team which comprises one person in charge of the referee assignment process, two persons in charge of the theoretical work on football rules and regulations, and two committee members of which one is responsible for the advancement of young referees and one for public relations.
[29] Ronald H. Coase (*1910 in Willesden, Great Britain) is a British economist, whose contributions to the topic of transaction costs which he explains in the so called "Coase-Theorem." Coase won the Nobel prize for this scientific work in 1991
[30] Cf. Coase (1937)
[31] Oliver E. Williamson (*1932 in Superior, U.SA.) is an American economist whose scientific focus is the New Institutional Economics, which he especially dealt with in his work "The Economic Institutions of Capitalism" (1985)
[32] Cf. Schuhmann (1987, p. 212). For further study: Cf. Erlei (2007, p. 13)
[33] For further study: Furubotn/Pejovich (1972, pp. 1137-1162)
[34] "Transaction costs are identifiable with costs that arise in connection with identifying, transferring and exercising disposal rights." Picot/Dietl (1990b, p. 178)
[35] For further study: Leipold (1975, p. 357-385)
[36] For further study: Picot/Dietl/Franck (1999, pp. 85-94)
[37] Cf. Pratt/Zeckhauser (1985)

As the interaction between the managing-committee and the referees also displays a form of Principal-Agent relationship the main elements of this theory now shall be illustrated by the following graphic.

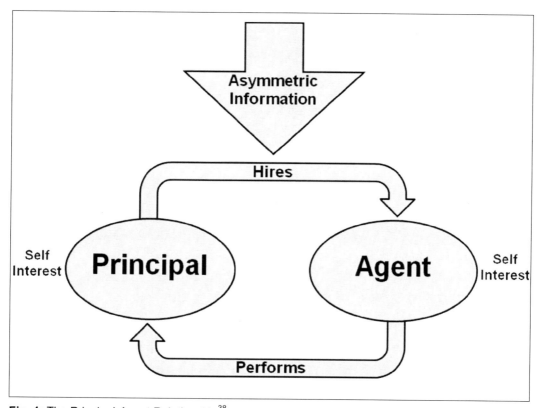

Fig. 1: The Principal-Agent Relationship[38]

The principal hires an agent to perform a certain task on behalf of the former. According to Gintis (2000), the principal`s payoff depends on the agent`s action.[39] The basic problem in this constellation is the asymmetric information between both parties involved, leading to agency costs. These comprise the costs for monitoring, bonding expenditures by the agent and the monetary equivalent between the best choice for the principal and the choice of the agent.[40] Moreover, the theory presumes that both players in this game do not have perfectly correlating self interests.

---

[38] Own Illustration
[39] Cf. Gintis, (2000, p. 332)
[40] Cf. Jensen/Meckling (1976)

According to Foss (1995), the agent might have intentions that do not allow for an optimal fulfillment of the principal's interests.[41] The incomplete information leads to three problems of which 'Hidden Characteristics' shall be considered first. When hiring an agent, the characteristics of the former may not be perfectly open for the principal. However, the principal has to mandate an agent to perform on his behalf. Due to the fact that the agent's characteristics cannot be perfectly assessed ex ante (before the contract is signed), the principal faces the threat of hiring an inappropriate candidate. The actual performance therefore can only be evaluated once the decision is made. Campbell (1995) illustrates this constellation with the help of an example that refers to a trip with a taxi.[42] The customer (principal) chooses a taxi without exactly knowing whether the taxi driver (agent) has invested in the maintenance of the car or not. A profit-maximizing taxi driver would tend to disobey necessary repair works in order to save money. Thus, the principal cannot be sure to sit in a safe car and has to rely on the taxi driver.

When assuming that an agent does not perform in the best interest of the principal (profit maximization), there arise two general forms of agency costs for the principal. In case, he wants to hire another agent, there are costs for the recruitment process (finding another taxi takes time) and for sacking a current agent (the customer has to pay a basic fee for calling a taxi, regardless if he chooses it for his trip or not). In case, he wants to go on with the current agent, he has to install mechanisms to improve the performance. This could be in form of training or coaching (not possible in the taxi example, as this interaction is a one-time relationship), which represent costs for the principal. In order to avoid problems resulting from 'Adverse Selection' (choosing an inappropriate agent) in advance, the principal can apply various instruments. 'Signaling Strategies' may help to reduce this 'Information Asymmetry'. This for example is often done in companies in the recruitment process. In order to minimize the risk of 'Adverse Selection', they often communicate the company's values openly in order to increase the chance of receiving applications from candidates that share these values and thus make a successful cooperation more probable. Another way to find an appropriate agent is to follow a 'Screening Strategy'.

---

[41] Cf. Foss (1995, p. 188)
[42] Cf. Campbell (1995, p. 8)

Conducting an assessment center and personal interviews can also increase the chance of finding the desired employee (agent). The third solution can be reached by the so called 'Self Selection' in which the principal designs various contracts from which the agent can choose. The choice of the latter then forebodes his intention. Referring to the recruitment process in a company, this means that the company offers the agent one contract with a fixed salary only and one with a fixed salary and a performance related salary component that result in a higher total salary if the agent performs well. According to the theory, an applicant who chooses the contract with the variable component is more intrinsically motivated and thus appropriate than an applicant who chooses the first contract. Akerlof (1970) was the first to develop a model that describes the problem of 'Adverse Selection'. With the 'Market of Lemons', he explained this problem with the example of used cars.[43]

The second problem, which arises in the context of a Principal-Agent relationship, is displayed by the 'Hidden Action'[44] and 'Hidden Information'. The former results from the fact that the principal cannot completely (only when accepting massive costs) monitor the agent`s action once he is hired. Indeed, he can assess the results, but does not have the means to evaluate the process connected with the outcome.[45] Thus, it cannot be figured out if the agent acts perfectly in his behavior. This is the will to maximize profits which - in accordance with Tirole (1988) - can be reached by reducing costs and increasing profits.[46] Referring back to the taxi example, 'Hidden Action' can be considered as follows. The principal wants to reach a certain destination as fast and as cheap as possible. The taxi driver as the agent on the other side wants to maximize his profit by not following the optimal route for the principal, but rather choosing a longer way in order to earn more money.[47]

Although the principal can control the quality of the output, it remains questionable if the quality and efficiency (less time, less material) has reached the maximal level possible under the given constraints. In order to answer these questions, the principal can install monitoring mechanisms to analyze where optimizing potential can be found or if the agent`s effort is satisfactory.

---

[43] Cf. Akerlof (1970, pp. 488-500)
[44] Cf. Foss (1995, p. 188)
[45] Cf. Rosen, (1993, pp. 83-84)
[46] Cf. Tirole (1988, p. 35)
[47] Cf. Campbell (1995, p. 7)

If the agent does not choose a high effort level, this is denoted as 'Moral Hazard'. In this case, the principal can introduce an incentive scheme that fosters the agent`s effort as his pay can be directly linked to the quantity and quality of the outcome. Again, these mechanisms are considered as forms of 'Agency Costs'.

In this context, another problem resulting from relationships with asymmetric information shall be introduced. Contrarily to the issue of 'Hidden Action', there might also occur problems resulting from 'Hidden Information'. This means that the principal can monitor the agent`s performance, but lacks the knowledge to evaluate the quality of the outcome. Referring to another example, this would mean that the principal can monitor the process of producing for example a personal computer, but lacks the knowledge to evaluate whether and how the quality could be improved. Again, this 'Information Asymmetry' causes costs for the principal. In this case, the principal may want to train himself in order to have a better understanding of personal computers. The costs for the training then represent 'Agency Costs'.

The third problem in a Principal-Agent relationship may arise even when the principal is able to monitor the agent and there is no 'Hidden Information'. However, this so called agent's 'Hidden Intention' might be different from what the principal wants and thus can bear unwanted consequences. More concretely, the agent might make use of a specific investment the principal makes (e.g. purchasing a machine with the only function of producing microchips for the personal computers). Presuming that the agent is the only person who is able to operate the machine, he might demand for a higher salary. As the principal depends on the knowledge of the agent in this case, he is more or less forced to comply, in order not to have purchased the machine without using it. This dependency is conferred to as the 'Hold Up' problem. However, if the principal does not comply, the machine represents a form of 'Sunk Costs'. Transferring this problem back to the taxi trip, the following behavior of the taxi driver represents a 'Hidden Intention'. Let us assume that the customer needs a taxi at night in order to catch his flight that is already booked (specific investment). The taxi driver knows that his customer has to catch his flight and is aware of the fact that his taxi is the only available one.

In this situation, he could charge a higher fee for the trip, as he is the only opportunity for the customer to get to the airport in time ('Hold Up'). Now, the customer can either pay the higher fee, or decide to miss his flight. In the latter case, the costs for the already booked flight represent 'Sunk Costs'.[48]

Besides the strategies mentioned, the literature on the topic of Principal-Agent relationships proposes further general approaches to solve the problems occurring. Bureaucratic control, information systems and incentives are the most prominent ones. An effective organizational culture, trust and a good reputation might also be a good basis for a well-functioning relation between the principal and the agent.[49] The effectiveness and appropriateness of those mechanisms in context of the case will be evaluated in the further course of this thesis. In a next step, Becker`s Deterrence Hypothesis will be introduced to create a basis for the analysis of punishment in this case.

4.2 The Deterrence Hypothesis

In 1968, Gary S. Becker[50] developed the Deterrence Hypothesis by analyzing the relationship between crime and the economic costs of law enforcement which include the costs of chasing and convicting the criminal. According to Becker and Landes (1974), the law shall only be enforced as long as this relationship is rational from an economic point of view.[51] In his hypothesis, Becker therefore neglects psychological and social traits that might also play a role in the decision process of a prospective delinquent to commit a crime or not. The basic finding from Becker`s analysis of crime in the U.S.A. ('United States of America') and the respective costs is that the severity and probability of a punishment are the decisive factors of deterring people from illegal behavior. In reference to Becker (1968), the crime rates decrease as the aforementioned factors increase.[52]

---

[48] Cf. Campbell (1995, pp. 7-8)
[49] For further study: Eisenhardt (1989, pp. 57-74)
[50] Gary Stanley Becker (* 2 December, 1930) is an American economist who was awarded the Nobel Prize in Economics in 1992 for his scientific research on investments in human capital, behavior of the family (or household), including distribution of work and allocation of time in the family, crime, punishment and discrimination on the markets for labor and goods.
[51] Cf. Becker/Landes (1974, p. 2)
[52] Cf. Becker (1968, pp. 169-217)

Zimring/Hawkins (1973) follow a more detailed distinction of the deterrence hypothesis and differentiate between the 'Absolute' and 'Marginal Deterrence':

> *"The problem of absolute deterrence relates to the question, Does this particular criminal sanction deter? The problem of marginal deterrence relates to such questions as, Would a more severe penalty attached to this criminal prohibition more effectively deter? In the capital punishment debate the issue is not that of absolute deterrence-whether the death penalty is a deterrent. It is that of marginal deterrence-whether it is a more effective deterrent than the alternative sanction of long imprisonment."*[53]

It becomes obvious that 'Marginal Deterrence' examines the implication of the severity of a punishment on the level of crime, whereas the 'Absolute Deterrence' refers to the most effective form of punishment for a specific kind of criminal behavior. The formal model describing the Deterrence Hypothesis shall be introduced in the following. According to Becker, persons develop expectations in regard to the gain of a possible crime. This means that they judge the value of the potential booty, the probability of being caught and convicted and the severity of the punishment. If the persons realize that this gain is higher than the gain from another, legal activity, they will commit the crime and will discard this plan if this is not the case.[54] The expected gain from committing a crime can be described as follows:[55]

$$EU_i = (1-p_i) * U_i (Y_i) + p_i * U_i (Y_i-f_i)$$

With:

U_i: Utility function (gain);

Y_i: Value of the illegal booty (monetary and/or psychological);

p_i: The probability of being convicted;

f_i: The monetary equivalent of the punishment;

Thus, the crime will be committed as long as $EU_i > 0$.

---

[53] Cf. Zimring/Hawkins (1973)
[54] Cf. Brier/Feinberg (1980, p. 153)
[55] Cf. Becker (1968, pp. 169-217)

Becker says that the expected gain from a crime decreases with an increased probability of being convicted and/or an increased punishment. This leads to the following functions:

$$\partial EU_i / \partial p_i = U * (Y_i - f_i) - U_i*(Y_i) < 0 \text{ and } \partial EU_i / \partial f_i = -p_i U *_i (Y_i - f_i) < 0$$

Becker furthermore tries to determine the number of a person's crimes in one period with the following approach:

$$O_j = O_j (p_j; f_j; u_j)$$

With:

O_j: The number of crimes committed by a person in one period;

p_j: The probability of being convicted per offense;

f_j: The fine per offense;

u_j: A portmanteau variable for other factors that influence the delinquency of person, such as income and general willingness to commit a crime;

Basing on the assumption that $\partial EU_i / \partial p_i < 0$ and $\partial EU_i / \partial f_i < 0$, the following formal approach is consequently valid as well:

$$O_i / \partial p_i < 0 \text{ and } \partial O_i / \partial f_i < 0$$

This shows that with an increasing probability of being convicted or a higher level of punishment, the personal 'crime rate' decreases as the expected gain of crimes is reduced. The model can be transferred to the entire society given that the preconditions for an aggregated 'function of choices' for the individual are met.

$$O = O*(p; f; u),$$

for which the same effects of *p* and *f* can be assumed.

This function is the core of Becker`s Deterrence Hypothesis, because it provides the state with the means **p** and **f**. Those support the steering of the criminality level with regard to the social costs. Becker`s intention was to set up a model framework to determine the level of criminality, minimizing the social costs.

The state reaches this by optimizing the loss function (with regard to monetary aspects):

L = D(O) + C(p, O) + bpfO,

With:

D('): The difference between the victim`s loss and the delinquent`s gain;

C('): The costs of law enforcement;

bpfO: A term representing the social costs of the conviction;

The following graph illustrates this issue.

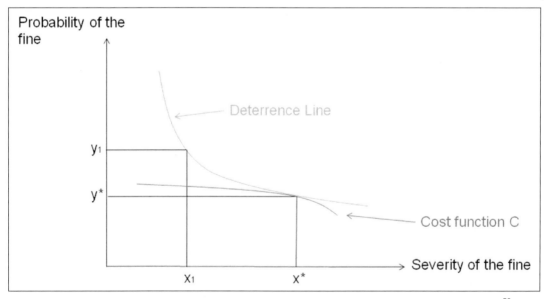

Fig. 2: Relation between the Probability/Severity of the Fine and the Costs of Law Enforcement[56]

The figure illustrates how the probability and the severity of the fine on the one hand and the cost function of the law enforcement on the other hand correspond.

---

[56] Own illustration, in accordance to Funk (2001, p. 25)

The deterrence line (green) shows the combination between probability and severity of a fine leading to a constant level of crime. The cost function C (red) shows the realizable combinations of probability and severity with a given constant budget for law enforcement. The optimal (and in this case only) combination is determined by the intersection of the deterrence line and the cost function (in this example **x*y***).

4.3 Motivation and Punishment in Scientific Literature

Undoubtedly, there has been done much work on the topic of motivation in economist literature. Abraham Maslow`s Needs Hierarchy, for example, represents a holistic approach to systematically illustrate different levels of human motivation. Morgan (1943) refers to Maslow when saying that human motivation depends on a hierarchy of needs, shown in the following graphic.[57]

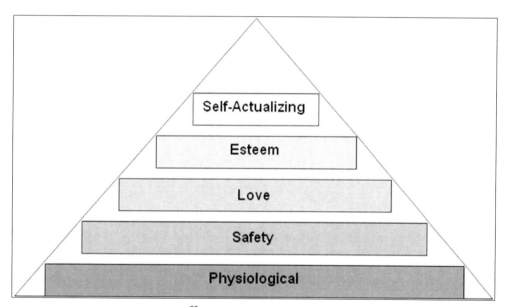

Fig. 3: Maslow`s Needs Hierarchy[58]

Maslow defines several levels that satisfy the different human needs. 'Physiological Needs' are the most basic form and can be satisfied by salaries and wages that are perceived as adequate. Moreover, providing a safe and comfortable working place may help to satisfy this need.

---

[57] Cf. Morgan (1943, p. 36)
[58] Own Illustration, in accordance to Maslow (1943, pp. 370-396)

'Safety' as the second hierarchical level can be reached by introducing pension and health care plans and job tenure in an organization. In order to fulfill the 'Love' demands, social facilities in an organization may be offered in order to create an environment that allows for social interaction with colleagues. Creating jobs that comprise autonomy, responsibility, and personal control as well as providing incentives for extraordinary performance serve as means to appeal to the 'Esteem Needs' of people. The most abstract needs level is the self-actualization of an individual, which can be reached by encouraging the employee's commitment.[59] Finally, it is important to know that these needs are not universally accepted. Negandhi and Savara (1989) for example utter a more distinctive opinion on this issue.

> *"There may not be a need hierarchy which applies to everyone; hierarchies do exist within individuals, however. The ability to motivate an individual depends on one's awareness of that individual's need hierarchy."*[60]

Another general approach to assess human motivation is delivered by Victor Vroom's Expectancy Theory. According to the theory, people will do things that attract them, avoid actions that may have negative consequences for them and ignore things that seem to be neither positive nor negative.[61] The following illustration shows the basic aspects of Vroom's theory.

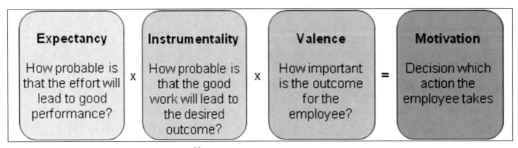

Fig. 4: Vroom's Expectancy Theory[62]

The pillar 'Expectancy' on the one hand describes the probability that a certain effort chosen by an individual leads to a good performance.

---

[59] Cf. Morgan (1943, p. 37)
[60] Negandhi/Savara (1989, p. 93)
[61] Cf. Atchison/Hill (1978, p. 188)
[62] Own Illustration, in accordance to Latham (2007, p. 46)

'Instrumentality' on the other hand refers to the question if the good work also leads to a desired outcome, such as a reward.[63] The value of the action's outcome for the individual is described as 'Valence'. These three pillars in the end result in the 'Motivation' of the respective person. As can be derived from the illustration, the level of motivation is the result of a multiplication which means that the higher the single pillars are rated, the higher the level of motivation is accordingly.

Obviously, the foregone theories deliver basic approaches to human motivation and also show how important the outcome of a performed task can be. In order to concretize these basic findings for the football referees` case, two papers on the topic of rewarding or punishing certain actions and the results from doing so will now be presented. In their paper "Motivation Crowding Theory: A Survey of Empirical Evidence" (Revised Version, 2001), Bruno S. Frey and Reto Jegen refer to the impact of external rewards on the motivation of human beings.[64] They show that offering a monetary reward for performing a specific task under certain conditions may undermine the intrinsic motivation of a person and therefore have an opposite effect from the intended one. Frey/Jegen find that the effects of external interventions on intrinsic motivation can be ascribed to two psychological processes of which 'Impaired self-determination' is the first one. The notion basically says that if a person considers an external intervention as a limiting influence in regard to the self-determination, extrinsic control mechanisms substitute the intrinsic motivation of the respective person. This means that the external pressure to behave in a certain way leads to a perceived extreme justification if the person`s level of intrinsic motivation remains stable. 'Impaired self-esteem' describes the negative consequences from not acknowledging a person`s action at all. This leads to a decreased level of intrinsic motivation as the person considers the value of his/her performed task to be not appreciated and thus not valuable at all. According to that, external interventions increase - or according to Frey/Jegen crowd in - intrinsic motivation if the respective person considers them as supportive. However, they crowd out (decrease) motivation if they are perceived as controlling.[65]

---

[63] Cf. Massie (1979, p. 144)
[64] Cf. Frey/Jegen (2001)
[65] Cf. Ibid.

In their paper, the authors also name various examples for motivation crowding theory stemming from circumstantial, laboratory and field evidence. One example is the introduction of a fine for parents who pick their children up too late from the daycare center. In a first step, the number of late parents over a certain period was elaborated. In a second step, a high monetary fine for collecting the children late was installed. After a short period of time, the number of late parents increased dramatically as the fine transforms the relationship between parents and teachers from a non-monetary into a monetary one. The parents` intrinsic motivation to keep to the time schedules therefore is reduced and the parents consider the teachers to be 'paid' for the inconvenience of having to stay longer. The paper in the end concludes that there really is strong empirical evidence for the motivation crowding theory, but still leaves room for further research.[66]

Besides Frey/Jegen, there are further authors who did research on motivational topics. Ronald Bénabou and Jean Tirole did further research on the effect of rewards and punishments onto intrinsic motivation and the perception of a specific task. In their paper "Intrinsic and Extrinsic Motivation" (2000), the authors define their focus of work as follows:

> *"Should a child be rewarded for passing an exam, or paid to read a book? What impact do empowerment and monitoring have on employees` morale and productivity? Does receiving help boost or hurt self-esteem? Why do incentives work well in some contexts, but appear counterproductive in others? Why do people sometimes undermine the self-confidence of others on whose effort and initiative they depend?"[67]*

The authors study these questions against the background of an agent with an imperfect self-knowledge and an informed principal who can offer different types of incentives. It is elaborated that rewards and punishments can often be counterproductive as they may subvert the agent`s intrinsic motivation. In many cases, extrinsic influences affect the agent`s perception of a task and his own skills. In this case, rewards are only little effective in a short-term view and even counterproductive in the long-term view.

---

[66] For further study: Frey/Jegen (2000)
[67] Bénabou/Tirole (2000, p. 489)

Bénabou and Tirole furthermore show that it is neither always advantageous for the principal to delegate work and thus demonstrate trust in the agent, nor exclusively right to find excuses for an agent`s failure. Moreover, it is elaborated that the means of rewarding and punishing strongly depend on the information the principal and the agent have and furthermore on the surrounding conditions.

5 Referees in non-professional football – The District of Guetersloh

This part of the thesis aims at applying the theoretical findings and the results from the questionnaire to the football referees in the district of Guetersloh. In order to understand the context, both the referees` organization and the current problems will be illustrated in the following section.

5.1 Facts and Figures

The district of Guetersloh in North Rhine-Westphalia has 353,944 inhabitants and an area of 967.19 km².[68] The following statistic sheds light on the number of football clubs and male members in the district.[69]

Male	Active Members	Number of Teams
Juniors (Age up to 6)	416	34
F-Juniors (Age 7-8)	804	67
E-Juniors (Age 9-10)	1,071	76
D-Juniors (Age 11-12)	1,077	59
C-Juniors (Age 13-14)	885	42
B-Juniors (Age 15-16)	881	35
A-Junior (Age 17-18)	675	31
TOTAL JUNIORS (MALE)	**5,809**	**344**
Seniors (Age 19-31)	2,160	86
Seniors (Age 32-39)	1,061	22
Seniors (Age > 40)	1,304	17
TOTAL SENIORS (MALE)	**4,525**	**125**
TOTAL MALE	**10,334**	**469**

Fig. 5: Overview - Male Football Players in the District of Guetersloh

---

[68] Effective Date: 12/31/2008. Source: https://www.landesdatenbank.nrw.de
[69] Effective Date: 12/31/2008

There are about 10,000 active male football players of which 56% are juniors. The E-Juniors (aged seven to eight) and D- Juniors (aged nine to ten) represent the largest group within the male juniors. However, it becomes obvious that the seniors at the age of 19 to 31 years (more than 2,000 members) are by far the biggest group of male football players. Furthermore, it can be seen that the number of junior teams (344) exceeds the number of senior teams (125) significantly although the amount of players is similar. The main reason for this difference lies in the team size of junior teams. In contrast to the seniors, where eleven players constitute a team, the junior teams (up to the age of 10) consist of seven players. D- and C-Juniors can play either in a league with eleven players or seven players. As a result, there are significantly more teams in the junior segment than in the senior segment. Having illustrated facts and figures concerning the male football players, the focus shall now be set on the females in the district of Guetersloh.[70]

Female	Active Members	Number of Teams
Juniors (Age up to 12)	291	14
Juniors (Age 13-14)	280	14
Juniors (Age 15-16)	195	16
TOTAL JUNIORS (FEMALE)	766	44
Seniors (Age 17-30)	214	11
Seniors (Age 31-39)	34	0
Seniors (Age > 40)	15	0
TOTAL SENIORS (FEMALE)	263	11
TOTAL FEMALE	1,029	55

Fig. 6: Overview - Female Football Players in the District of Guetersloh

The number of female football players is significantly lower than the number of male players. Only about nine per cent of the total football players in the district are female. Female players aged over 30 are not organized in separate teams and thus play in teams with other senior females. Due to the low number of females, there are no leagues on district level for them.

---

[70] Effective Date: 12/31/2008

The existing female teams therefore are assigned to a joint league with the neighboring district of Bielefeld. Figure 7 shows which divisions for male teams exist and how the competition is organized in the district of Guetersloh.

Division	Number of Groups	Number of Teams
Seniors „Kreisliga A"	1	16
Seniors „Kreisliga B"	2	32
Seniors „Kreisliga C"	2	33
First Division A-Juniors	1	12
Second Division A-Juniors	1	9
First Division B-Juniors	1	12
Second Division B-Juniors	2	23
First Division C-Juniors	1	12
Second Division C-Juniors	2	20
	Total: 13	Total: 169

Fig. 7: Divisions and Teams in the District of Guetersloh

In order to maintain a functioning league system, neutral referees are assigned to the weekly matches. In total, 133 active referees are available. 18 passive referees currently cannot be assigned to matches for various reasons. According to the league system with promotion and relegation, the referees can also qualify for different leagues. The current classification of referees is shown in the following table.

Division	Number of Referees
Seniors „NRW-Liga" (formerly „Oberliga")	0
Seniors „Westfalenliga" (formerly „Verbandsliga")	4
Seniors „Landesliga"	2
Seniors „Bezirksliga"	14
Seniors „Kreisliga A"	25
Seniors „Kreisliga B"	28
Seniors „Kreisliga C"	40
Juniors (in the district only)	20

Fig. 8: Referee Classification in the District of Guetersloh

The major part of referees is exclusively active in the lower divisions in Guetersloh whereas only 15% can be assigned to higher divisions in the area of the FLVW ('Fußball- und Leichtathletik-Verband Westfalen'). It is also striking that there is no referee in the professional divisions of the DFB ('Deutscher Fußball Bund').[71] Figure 9 will give an impression of the referees` age structure.

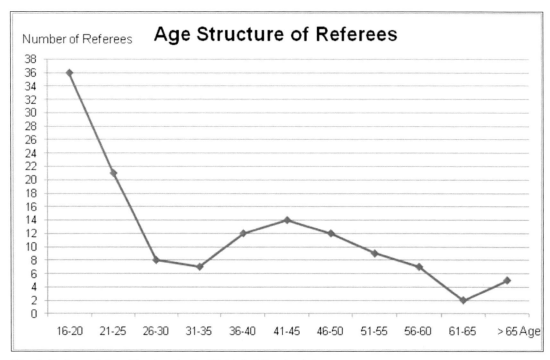

Fig. 9: Referees` Age Structure in the District of Guetersloh

As can be seen, many young referees are active in the district of Guetersloh. However, as the referees get older, the number of referees significantly decreases. As a result, the total number only hardly suffices to assign a referee to every match which, in return, represents one major problem of the KSA.

---

[71] In this case, the "Regionalliga", the "3. Liga", the "2. Bundesliga" and the "1. Bundesliga" will be considered as professional leagues. This definition also corresponds to the classification of the DFB.

5.2 Organization

In the following section, it will be explained which structures exist and how the referees are organized. This comprises the description of the recruitment process, the intention of the monthly meetings, the annual test and the referee assignment procedure.

5.2.1 Structures

The K34 (district of Guetersloh)[72] is one of thirty-three districts in the area of the FLVW, which - together with the FVN ('Fußball-Verband Niederrhein') and the FVM ('Fußball-Verband Mittelrhein') - forms the WFLV ('Westdeutscher Fußball- und Leichtathletikverband'). The WFLV again is one of twenty-one regional associations in Germany. More than 18,000 athletes are organized in the district of Guetersloh, splitting-up into the segments football (juniors and seniors), athletics, recreational sport, mass sport and football referees. The sport in Guetersloh is supervised by the sports committee of the district.[73]

The 151 active and passive referees are directed by the KSA ('Kreis-Schiedsrichterausschuss'). The chairman leads the committee, which consists of two coaches, who are responsible for the theoretical qualification, one person who is in charge of the referee assignments and three committee members of which one is responsible for PR ('Public Relations') and two for the education of young referees. All of them have been or still are active referees.

---

[72] "K" is the abbreviation for the German word "Kreis", which means "district". The number represents the respective district in the FLVW. Although there are only thirty-three districts in this area, the numbers range from one to thirty-four. This is due to the fact, that the districts were reorganised and K9 was affiliated to an existing district. However, the number "34" remained.

[73] The original German expression is „Kreisvorstand Guetersloh". This committee consists of nine members. There is a representative for mass sports, athletics, youth sports, the football referees, one assessor, a treasurer, an executive secretary and one honorary member. The committee is presided by a chairman

5.2.2 The Referee Constitution

The district of Guetersloh is assigned to the FLVW and therefore has to adapt to the existing rules and regulations of the association. Besides clauses for the youth, athletics, and finances, there is an explicit constitution for the referees, which consists of the following contents. [74]

Paragraph	Contents
§ 1	General Clauses
§ 2	Rights and Duties during the Match
§ 3	Rights and Duties after the Match
§ 4	Kick-Off in case of unpunctual End of the preceded Match
§ 5	Absence of the Referee
§ 6	Assignment, Rejection and Deletion of Referees
§ 7	Jurisdiction against Referees
§ 8	Punishment Authorities against Referees
Appendix Referee Constitution	Teaching and examination clauses, performance classes
Youth Referee Constitution	General Clauses, Qualification, Assignment, Development

Fig. 10: Referee Constitution

The constitution is not handed out to the referees and thus not known by everyone. It is rather considered as a guideline and the referees` compliance is taken for granted.

5.2.3 Recruitment Process

In order to maintain a functioning competition with neutral referees, the FLVW has adopted various rules and regulations. One of these obliges the clubs to detach a certain number of referees that depends on the number of Senior, A- and B- Junior teams and their respective division. The exact clauses can be found as "3-Stufen-Plan"[75] in the provision of the FLVW.

---

[74] The complete Constitution (effective Date January 1999) is to be found in the digital appendix
[75] For further study: „Durchführungsbestimmungen zu § 30 Abs. 3 – 5 SpO/WFLV" or www.flvw.de

The detachment scheme of referees is as follows: Teams in professional leagues, the "Regionalliga", the "NRW-Liga" ('North Rhine Westfalian', formerly "Oberliga"), the "Westfalenliga" (formerly "Verbandsliga") and the "Landesliga" of male seniors have to detach three referees per team. Teams of the female "Bundesliga" and "Regionalliga" have to detach three referees per team. Teams in the male A- and B-Juniors-"Bundesliga" and "Westfalenliga" also have to detach three referees per team. Moreover, teams of the female senior "Verbandsliga", "Landesliga", "Bezirks- und "Kreisligen" have to detach one referee. This is also valid for teams in the male seniors "Bezirksliga", "Kreisliga A, B, C and D" and teams in the "Landesliga", "Bezirksliga" and "Kreisliga" of the male A-/B-Juniors.

If a club cannot manage to detach the required number of referees, the consequences of the "3-Stufen-Plan" come into play. These are illustrated in the following overview.

Step	Consequences
1	**Seasonal fine that is dependent on the division of the first team:** - Becomes effective in the first year - Teams in professional leagues, the "Regionalliga", the "NRW-Liga", the "Westfalenliga": **EUR 250.00** - Teams of the "Landesliga" and the "Bezirksliga": **EUR 200.00** - Teams of the "Kreisliga A, B, C and D": **EUR 150.00**
2	**Ban: No organization of tournaments** - Becomes effective as soon as the club does not accomplish the required number of referees by 60% in the second season - Club anniversaries are an exception
3	**Disqualification/Relegation of a team** - Becomes effective in the third season if the number of required referees is not reached by 40% - Relegation of the club's male team in the lowest league - Deprivation of the championship title if a club has only one team that won the title - Deprivation of the team in the lowest division if a club disregards the clauses in three subsequent seasons

Fig. 11: The "3-Stufen-Plan"

Generally, the clubs announce referee candidates which have to pass an aspirant seminar to become an official referee. However, the KSA cannot influence the clubs' choice. The education consists of eight meetings lasting two hours each, in which the football rules are conveyed. The seminar concludes with a test consisting of a theoretical and a running part. In regard to the theoretical examination, ten multiple-choice questions have to be answered.

For each question, there are three answer options which the aspirant has to choose the correct one from. Additionally, twenty questions have to be answered in written form. The aspirants have to reach at least fifty points out of sixty in order to pass this part of the examination.

The running test consists of the following three disciplines.

- **Male Referees**
    1. 50 meters (max. 9.5 Seconds)
    2. 100 meters (max. 16.6 Seconds
    3. 1,000 meters (max. 5:30 Minutes)

- **Female Referees**
    1. 50 meters (max.11.0 Seconds)
    2. 100 meters (max. 19.0 Seconds)
    3. 1,000 meters (max. 6:00 Minutes)

If the aspirants pass this exam, they are official referees and can be assigned to matches in junior divisions.

5.2.4 Monthly Meetings and Annual Test

The referees are obliged to attend monthly meetings of two hours on a regular basis. The intention of this mandatory event is to inform the referees about news and changes in the clauses and furthermore to improve and brush up their knowledge in terms of rules and regulations. The meeting also serves as a forum and means to boost the referees` performance. In order to allow for a more purposeful work, the KSA decided to split up the referees into three groups. The first group consists of the young referees who have been active for less than two years. Their meetings aim at facilitating and improving the beginning of their career. Thus, rather basic questions and advice are in the focus of interest and a forum with practical questions and referees` experiences shall be created. Referees who are active on district level represent the second group. The focus of interest here is to be seen in the theoretical education as these colleagues tend to neglect the regular work on rules and regulations.

The referees who are assigned to matches in higher divisions of the regional association find themselves in the third group which is intended to improve the referee`s performance during matches. This refers to the referee`s behavior in stress situations, tactical tips and especially the improvement of the teamwork with the assistant referees.

Besides the meetings for the specific groups, all referees meet twice a year in order to create an atmosphere of fellowship and a shared identity. In addition to the monthly meetings, the annual test is also mandatory for every referee in Guetersloh. It consists of a theoretical test with thirty questions on the football rules and a running test with three disciplines. The requirements to pass the test comply with the respective division in which the referee is active. With the results, the KSA wants to measure the referees` performance level, but also to elaborate which colleagues are worthy of promotion. The annual test consequently serves as an objective tool to decide about promotion and relegation of referees on district level.

5.2.5 Referee Assignment Process

The referees are assigned to matches according to their qualification. This means that a referee cannot be assigned to a match in a division that is higher than his qualification. However, they can also be told off to a match in a lower league. As a result of a recent reform, the assignments now are made via e-mail. This means that the person in charge of the assignments invites the referees to their matches with an e-mail that the respective arbitrator has to confirm by clicking on a specific link in the mail.

An exemplary assignment per e-mail is shown below. The link for the confirmation can be found in blue color at the end of the mail.

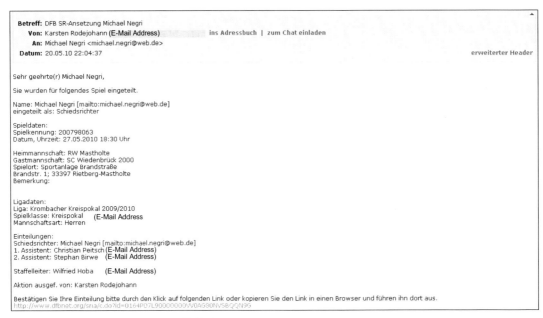

Betreff: DFB SR-Ansetzung Michael Negri
  Von: Karsten Rodejohann (E-Mail Address)   ins Adressbuch | zum Chat einladen
   An: Michael Negri <michael.negri@web.de>
Datum: 20.05.10 22:04:37   erweiterter Header

Sehr geehrte(r) Michael Negri,

Sie wurden für folgendes Spiel eingeteilt.

Name: Michael Negri [mailto:michael.negri@web.de]
eingeteilt als: Schiedsrichter

Spieldaten:
Spielkennung: 200798063
Datum, Uhrzeit: 27.05.2010 18:30 Uhr

Heimmannschaft: RW Mastholte
Gastmannschaft: SC Wiedenbrück 2000
Spielort: Sportanlage Brandstraße
Brandstr. 1; 33397 Rietberg-Mastholte
Bemerkung:

Ligadaten:
Liga: Krombacher Kreispokal 2009/2010
Spielklasse: Kreispokal   (E-Mail Address)
Mannschaftsart: Herren

Einteilungen:
Schiedsrichter: Michael Negri [mailto:michael.negri@web.de]
1. Assistent: Christian Peitsch (E-Mail Address)
2. Assistent: Stephan Birwe   (E-Mail Address)

Staffelleiter: Wilfried Hoba   (E-Mail Address)

Aktion ausgef. von: Karsten Rodejohann

Bestätigen Sie Ihre Einteilung bitte durch den Klick auf folgenden Link oder kopieren Sie den Link in einen Browser und führen ihn dort aus.
http://www.dfbnet.org/sria/c.do?id=0164P07L90000000VVOAGS0NVSBQQN9G

Fig. 12: Referee Assignment via E-Mail

The higher the division, the more short-term the assignments are made. This means that a referee in the "Westfalenliga" normally receives this mail seven days before the match, whereas the colleagues in the "Kreisliga" know about their assignments several weeks before the actual match. If a referee is not able to take over a match, he has to announce this as early as possible in order to allow the person in charge of the referee assignment to reshuffle matches or find a substitute.

5.2.6 Remuneration

Similarly to the away team, the referees have to travel to their matches. They receive 0.30 cents per driven kilometer. In the higher divisions, where assistant referees are provided, 0.32 cents per kilometer are paid if two persons are in one car and 0.34 cents per kilometer if all three referees travel together. In addition to this money, charges are paid for the matches according to the respective division. The following overview shows how much money is paid in the different divisions.

Division	Referee	Assistant Referee
Male Juniors		
A-Juniors "Westfalenliga"	23.00 Euros	11.50 Euros
A-Juniors "Landesliga"	17.00 Euros	8.50 Euros
A-Juniors "Bezirksliga"	11.00 Euros	7.00 Euros
A-Juniors "Kreisliga"	10.00 Euros	7.00 Euros
B-Juniors "Westfalenliga"	17.00 Euros	8.50 Euros
B-Juniors "Landesliga"	11.00 Euros	7.00 Euros
B-Juniors "Bezirksliga"	8.50 Euros	6.00 Euros
B-Juniors "Kreisliga"	8.00 Euros	6.00 Euros
C-Juniors "Regionalliga"	18.00 Euros	9.00 Euros
C-Juniors "Landesliga"	8.50 Euros	6.00 Euros
C-Juniors "Bezirksliga"	7.00 Euros	5.00 Euros
C-. D-. E- .F-Juniors "Kreisliga"	6.00 Euros	
Female Juniors		
B-Juniors "Westfalenliga"	11.00 Euros	
B-Juniors "Bezirksliga"	8.50 Euros	

Division	Referee	Assistant Referee
Male Seniors		
"NRW-Liga" (formerly „Oberliga")	50.00 Euros	30.00 Euros
"Westfalenliga" (formerly „Verbandsliga")	33.00 Euros	17.00 Euros
"Landesliga"	28.00 Euros	17.00 Euros
"Bezirksliga"	20.00 Euros	14.00 Euros
"Kreisliga A"	18.00 Euros	14.00 Euros
"Kreisliga B"	16.00 Euros	-
"Kreisliga C"	16.00 Euros	-
Over 32 years old / Over 40 years old	16.00 Euros	-
Cup matches on FLVW level	33.00 Euros	17.00 Euros
Cup matches on district level	20.00 Euros	16.00 Euros
Female Seniors		
"Regionalliga"	25.00 Euros	13.00 Euros
"Verbandsliga"	15.00 Euros	11.50 Euros
"Landesliga"	14.50 Euros	10.00 Euros
"Bezirksliga"	14.00 Euros	-
"Kreisliga"	13.00 Euros	-
Cup matches on FLVW level	15.00 Euros	11.50 Euros
Cup matches on district level	13.00 Euros	-

Fig. 13: Referee Remuneration

Referees who are assigned to a tournament receive 7.00 Euros an hour.

5.2.7 Promotion/Relegation

The promotion and relegation system on district level allows for a flexible classification of referees. The main criteria for the classification up to the "Kreisliga A" are a constant participation in the monthly meetings, the attendance of the yearly test, reliability, and the willingness to take over additional matches. The KSA then decides about the referees` promotion and delegation at the end of every season individually. In exceptional cases, the classification of single referees is made during the season. A promotion to the "Bezirksliga" is only possible if the KSA nominates the candidate and announces him or her to the FLVW. This means that the referee has to pass a running test and a theoretical test with thirty questions. If he or she is successful, the candidate is promoted. The step into the next division ("Landesliga") is more difficult. The KSA has a certain contingent of referees that can be nominated for a pool of candidates from the entire FLVW area. At the beginning of a season, the referees have to pass an entrance test. If so, they are monitored and judged during their matches by representatives of the FLVW. Normally, eight assessments per referee are made during one season. The criteria for the assessment of the referee`s performance during a match can be seen in the following official document.

Fig. 14: Referee Assessment Sheet, Page 1

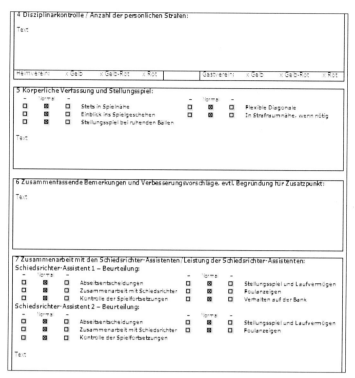

Fig. 15: Referee Assessment Sheet, Page 2

After half of the season, the referees whose grades are below the average of the respective are dismissed from the pool. The best referees then are promoted to the "Westfalenliga" at the end of the season. The influence of the KSA on the candidates for the pools is limited as all candidates for the promotion to the next division ("NRW-Liga") are nominated by the FLVW. The promotion procedure is similar for all non-professional leagues in the FLVW area. Only the requirements of the theoretical and running test become more demanding the higher the division is.

At the end of each season, the referees have to pass a final examination consisting of a theoretical test and a running test. The requirements again are oriented on the respective division. Only if the candidate passes this test, he or she is allowed to remain in this division in the following season. A referee is automatically relegated to the next lower division if he or she does not pass this test or is older than 47 years. However, the age restriction is only valid for divisions above the "Bezirksliga". Besides these external restrictions, the referees can of course also be voluntarily relegated to a lower division.

5.3 Display of the Problems

The KSA is faced with various problems concerning the work with the referees in the district of Guetersloh. On the one hand, the major part of the 133 active referees does not attend the monthly meetings and thus is not informed about recent changes in the rules and regulations. As a consequence, their performance during the matches is insufficient which in return leads to problems between players, coaches, or club officials and the referee. On the other hand, the referees who attend the meetings often disturb the referent and show a lack of interest. Similar problems occur in regard to the annual test. Only few referees participate in this obligatory event and the performances of those are not satisfactory in most cases. Furthermore, many referees cancel their assignment to matches too short-termed and cause trouble for the person in charge of the referee assignments as he has to find another referee who takes over the respective match. In the context of matches, the KSA recently found out about several cases of fraud, referees were involved in. The KSA is aware of these problems for which motivational aspects seem to be the trigger. However, the referees` managing-committee has no information regarding the intrinsic motivation of its referees.

Additionally, the means of extrinsic motivation such as monetary reward and promotion in case of good performance do not seem to be effective. Furthermore, the current forms of punishing misbehavior are not efficient either as the fines for absenteeism during monthly meetings, but also the annual test do not have the desired outcome. Additionally, a relegation or dismissal often is impossible as there are not enough referees anyway. A dismissal therefore would lead to an even more striking lack of arbitrators and a threatened competition due to missing neutral referees. This trend is not in the KSA`s interest. Therefore, alternative solutions to increase the referees` motivation have to be found. The approaches then shall help to reduce the current problems and to increase the referee`s dedication to this honorary engagement. At the same time, it shall be investigated, which role punishment plays in the context. In order to do so, various hypotheses will be set up. Those shall be introduced below.

5.4 Hypotheses

In order to set up a framework for the analysis, various hypotheses in regard to motivational issues and forms of punishment were examined with the help of a questionnaire and the presented theories. However, the hypotheses do not serve as the exclusive means and are backed up by further findings of the analysis.

5.4.1 Motivational Issues

Basically, it can be assumed that the referees` motives differ according to their age. Old referees are considered to be rather intrinsically motivated. This means that the reasons for being a referee originate in the activity itself. Possible motives for intrinsically motivated referees are to stay healthy by exercising this activity, to develop one`s personality and to compensate for the stressful job. On the other hand, young referees may tend to be extrinsically motivated by influences such as payment, promotion and free access to matches in the area of the DFB.[76] Similarly to the differing motives for being a referee, it can be assumed that the reasons for both attending and being absent during the monthly meetings and the annual test differ according to the age. The referee`s division may also be an influencing factor for the shaping of the different motives. Furthermore, it can be assumed that the referees do not have a positive impression of the monthly meeting and the annual test. This could be consulted as one major reason for the low participation in these mandatory events.

5.4.2 Punishment/Fines

The current forms of punishment are generally not effective as they do not deter the referees from misbehaving. However, it may be assumed that the perception of punishment differs between young and old referees. This is, because young referees may be rather repelled by these forms of punishment as they do not want to jeopardize their career or pay a fine as they tend to be more insecure and motivated in comparison to the older, more experienced referees. Furthermore, the division the referees are qualified for may also affect their attitude towards fines.

---

[76] The free access refers to all matches from district level to the German Bundesliga. Every club in the first and second division is obliged to hold up to 300 free tickets available for referees. On presentation of the referee identification card, these tickets are handed over. However, the tickets cannot be reserved and are only available at the day of the respective match.

Referees in the "Kreisliga C" for example do not have to fear relegation, as they already find themselves in the lowest division. In addition to this assumption, old referees may be less deterred by a five Euro fine than their younger colleagues as they normally earn more money than their younger colleagues (e. g. pupils or students). Furthermore, it can be assumed that the referees do not consider a fine for not attending the meeting without excuse as justified. This might be, because they think that their voluntary activity as a referee already represents enough commitment which should not be punished. After having set up the hypotheses, the questionnaire study and its underlying circumstances shall be introduced.

5.5 The Questionnaire Study

In order to find out more about the referees` motives, interests and their attitude towards punishment, a questionnaire was set up. The findings shall serve as practical approaches to increase motivation and the effectiveness of fines in the case presented. In the following, this questionnaire shall be introduced. The questionnaire was distributed to the referees on district level and the young referees who passed their aspirants test less than two years ago at the beginning of the monthly meeting on Monday, September 7, 2009. The referees who are active in the higher division on FLVW level filled out the questionnaire at the beginning of the monthly meeting on Thursday, September 10, 2009. Before the referees started to answer the questionnaire, they were introduced to the procedure. Help and guidance were offered during the process time of maximal thirty minutes. Due to the fact that not every referee speaks English, the questionnaire was set up in German in order to minimize misunderstandings resulting from linguistic issues.

In the first section, personal data is gathered such as age, school education and profession. In the following section, the respondents provide information regarding their career as a referee. The questionnaire then refers to the underlying motives of being a referee. Section four and five examine the referees` attitude towards the monthly meetings as well as towards the annual test and the reasons for attendance, and for absence respectively. Likert Items with a five ordered response level ("Totally disagree" → "Rather disagree" → "Don´t know" → "Rather agree" → "Totally agree") are applied to measure those reasons in a detailed manner.

The aim of section six is to elaborate on the referees` opinion regarding punishment and fines for misbehavior by providing various statements, which the respondents can agree with, deny or leave undecided. Section 7.1 aims at inquiring the referees` attitude towards assistance during the matches via the same kind of Likert Items. In order to evaluate if and to what extent bribery plays a role in the non-professional football, the referees also are faced with respective questions and statements in section 7.2 of the questionnaire. The questionnaire then closes with a section in which the referees have the opportunity to utter wishes, criticism and remarks regarding the theoretical education, the assignments, the monthly meetings, the annual test, the KSA, their matches and experiences with violence and insults during matches.

In total, 62 questionnaires returned were returned of which two were not evaluable due to missing information. The answers were transferred to Microsoft Excel where they were encoded. The following table shows the answers and their respective code for the statistical analysis with the computer program.[77]

| Code | Answer/Option | | | |
	Likert Scale	Polar questions	Sex	Age
1	"Totally disagree"	"Yes"	"Female"	16-25
2	"Rather disagree"	"No"	"Male"	26-35
3	"Don`t know"	"Don`t know"	-	36-45
4	"Rather agree"	-	-	46-55
5	"Totally agree"	-	-	>55

Fig. 16: Overview: Codes for Statistical Analysis

Besides the various age classes, the referees were additionally divided according to the division they are active in. Those are youth divisions, district level and FLVW level. The referees` motives and their attitude towards punishment represent the focus of the analysis. Various multivariate regressions were conducted with age and the referees` division as independent variables.

---

[77] The program Stata/IC 10.0 for windows was used for the actual analysis

5.6   Results from the Questionnaire Study

For the purpose of examining the hypotheses' validity, the findings from the questionnaire will be displayed in this paragraph and then are compared with the assumptions made. The results will be split up into the pillars motivation, monthly meetings, annual test, punishment/fines, coaching, and bribery/game manipulation to provide a structured analysis.

5.6.1 Motivation

Regarding the referees motivation, various findings resulted from the questionnaire of which only the most significant ones will be named in the following. The motive of taking over responsibility on the field was rated the highest with an average score of 4.2 on the five-stepped Likert Scale. Another argument for being a referee is that they obviously feel happy and relieved after a satisfactory match.

The regression with the independent variables age and division with the dependent variable "I want to show who the boss of the match is" reveals that the older the referees are and the higher their division is, the less important this argument is for them. Besides these rather psychological motives, the referees also consider this activity as a means to stay in shape. Not surprisingly, the older the referees are, the higher they rate this statement. The motive of earning money is rated relatively high by the young referees, but the tendency towards a decreasing score by older referees in the end leads to a total average rating of 2.6. It is also evident that this reason is less important for referees who are active on FLVW level than for referees in the youth and senior divisions on district level. This allows for the interpretation that there is obviously no striking financial reason for being a referee in non-professional football. This impression is backed up by the finding that the argument of having the opportunity to eat and drink for free before and after a match is rated with the lowest score (1.6) in this section of the questionnaire. The statement "I am a referee, because this is my only hobby" was also rated relatively low. Therefore, it seems as if there also exist further activities in the referees' free time which may have a negative impact on their dedication to this activity. The statements of being a referee in order to let out one's frustration or because the clubs asked the people to become a referee were rated low and do not represent a significant influence.

Furthermore, the older the referees are, the less they consider the will to be promoted as far as possible and the reason of trying something new as decisive factors.

5.6.2 Monthly Meeting

Attending the monthly meetings is mandatory for the referees. However, many of them do not show up. It is therefore interesting to figure out how the referees think about monthly meetings. Their opinions might serve as an indicator where potential for improvement can be identified. As a possible consequence of changes regarding the meetings, the attendance might increase if those are perceived as advantageous.

As a result of the questionnaire, it becomes obvious that locating the meetings in the 'Spexarder Bauernhaus' is considered to be appropriate. This impression goes along with the perceived positive atmosphere during the meetings. Besides organizational aspects, the football rules are an important element of the monthly meetings. The way of presenting the theoretical contents is rated positively with a high average score of 4.1. Furthermore, the referees have the opinion that the duration of the theoretical part (one hour) shall neither be shorter nor longer. Additionally, the contents appear to be more interesting for the old persons than for the younger ones. However, differing wishes of the age classes can also be detected. The younger the referees are the more theoretical work in form of video sequences is desired, whereas the older colleagues are in favor of more tests on the rules. As can be seen, the referees rather have a positive opinion in regard to the monthly meeting which allows for the interpretation that the reason for the low participation must be found somewhere else.

Based on this positive perception of monthly meetings, the reasons for attending those, but also for absence will be examined in order to elaborate possible opportunities for improvement. The most relevant reasons for attending the monthly meeting are its obligatory character (average score 4.1) and the fact that the referees are interested in the theoretical contents (average score 4.1). Especially considering the referees' age it is apparent that the older the referees are, the more they think that the theoretical work is interesting, and the more they see the meeting as an opportunity to learn something new and to show their theoretical knowledge.

The fine for being absent without an excuse that is imposed on the referee`s club only slightly impacts the referees` decision to attend the meeting. This is also valid for the possible consequence to be assigned to less 'attractive' matches. As the reasons for attending the meetings have now been illustrated, it is also worthwhile to explain why the referees are absent without an excuse. Unfortunately, the results of the questionnaire do not allow for a valid statement in this regard as the average scores are not significant.

On the contrary, there are only some reasons which can be excluded with certainty. The referees neglect the statements of not attending the monthly meeting because they do not feel like participating in it and the assumption that they dislike the colleagues. Moreover, the missing opportunity of promotion and the oblivion of the appointment cannot be used as valid reasons. What all these statements have in common is that the younger colleagues rate them higher than the older ones. After having analyzed the referees` attitude towards the monthly meeting, the annual test shall now be regarded in the next step.

5.6.3 Annual Test

Besides all monthly meetings, the annual test represents the second obligatory event for the referees. Similarly to the monthly meeting, the motives for attendance and absence were analyzed. The results show that the duty to take part in the test has the highest score (4.2 on average). Further reasons with a significant shaping are that the referees want to figure out how good they really are (average score 3.9) and to prove their theoretical knowledge (average score 3.8). The regression of the motive to participate in order to be promoted and the age shows that this tendency decreases with growing age. This can also be observed with the motive to show ones abilities. In contrast to other statements, only one significant conclusion can be drawn regarding the reasons for not participating in the annual test. Obviously, the referees do not fear too many mistakes in the theoretical test on the rules (average score of 1.6).

5.6.4 Punishment and Fines

In contrast to the foregone sections of the questionnaire, the statements on punishment and fines were rated based on a three stepped scale with the options "Yes" (code 1) and "No" (code 2). The answer option "Don`t know" is ignored for this analysis as it does not allow for a rational interpretation and would additionally distort the average score. Consequently, the lower the average score is, the higher the agreement with the respective statement is. The lowest score and thus the most agreement was uttered concerning the statement "A fine for an unexcused absence on the annual test is justified", "The fine itself is appropriate"[78] and "The fines for an unexcused absence while the monthly meeting and the annual test are imposed consequently by the KSA". All statements were rated with an average score of 1.2. However, it has to be remarked that only 35 answers were given and taken into the calculation for the latter statement. The most disagreement is to be found with reference to the deterring effect of the fine itself. Following the referees` answers, the introduction of a monetary fine for not attending the annual test would not lead to a considerable increase in the number of participants. A similar tendency can be observed regarding the introduction of a fine for a late return of an assigned match. Due to the score of 1.6, it can be doubted that the implementation of a fine would have the desired effect of less delayed returns.

A basic precondition for a fine`s effectiveness is that the delinquent itself has to pay it. Due to bureaucratic simplicity, the referees` clubs are charged with the fine for the misbehavior of their referee. This means that the delinquents do not necessarily have to pay the fine. Consequently, it is of importance to analyze, how many referees actually have to refund the fines. With the help of the questionnaire, it was found out that only 32% (19 persons out of 60) really pay this fine. This finding is a possible explanation for the ineffectiveness of the current forms of punishment and shall be discussed in detail in the further course of this work.

---

[78] The fine for an unexcused absence on the day of the monthly meeting is five Euros. The referee's club is charged with this fine on a monthly basis by the KSA. The information is conveyed in the so called "Amtliche Mitteilung" which is an official document on a monthly basis that is free of charge for the clubs. The referee does not necessarily have to refund this amount.

5.6.5 Coaching

In order to improve the referees` performance during the matches, the KSA is currently thinking about introducing a coaching system for the referees. To learn more about the attitude towards this idea, the five-stepped Likert Scale was applied again. The analysis shows that the arbitrators would rather feel uncomfortable if they were coached and observed by the KSA (average score 2.0). What becomes obvious is the tendency of a decreasing score for the statement that other colleagues could provide oneself with useful tips with growing age of the respondents. The same tendency can be recognized for the statement that the referees would obey to the rules and regulations more precisely if the KSA was present to monitor them. Further results of the other statements do not show a significant tendency and can be disregarded.

5.6.6 Bribery / Game Manipulation

Game manipulation and bribery are currently much discussed topics in the media. Especially the professional football suffers from the manipulation of matches by both, players and referees. Although there is less money involved in the non-professional football, this development can also be identified in the amateur divisions. In order to assess the scope of game manipulation and bribery, the referees of Guetersloh were asked to what extent they have experience with this phenomenon. In order to receive honest answers, the questionnaire was set up on an anonymous basis. However, it still has to be remarked that not every referee might have replied truthfully. Following this assumption, the actual results might be even higher.

Six out of 60 referees (10%) admitted that they have changed a red card against a player into a sending-off due to the second yellow card in one match. This leads to the consequence that the respective player is not suspended from following matches. The reasons for this behavior might be pressure on the referee or also a monetary compensation. However, those reasons were not covered with the questionnaire and therefore are not backed up empirically. The number of referees who were offered money for purposely made decisions in favor of a certain team is even higher. 18% percent of the referees confirmed to have acted in this way. The amount offered for this conscious preference of a team ranges from ten to three hundred Euros.

6 Case Solution

In this section, the case will be analyzed by addressing the various problems separately. This will be done with the theoretical basis and the findings from the empirical study. When doing so, it has to be remarked that the Principal-Agent Theory is concerned with problems that result from information asymmetries in a relationship of mutual dependencies. In most cases, this relationship is based on a contract which determines the rights and duties of both parties involved. When analyzing the referees` case it must be considered that such a contract is currently not in place.

6.1 Missing Quantity of Referees

Similar to other honorary posts, the KSA faces a lack of persons that are willing to become a referee. Currently, there are 133 active referees and 18 passive members. This number already is alarming as the number of matches where an official referee is required is similar to the number of referees that actually are available. In some cases, one referee has to be assigned to two or three matches at one weekend. In order to stop this negative trend, immediate action has to be taken. This problem is not directly considered in the context of the Principal-Agent Theory. Still, there are possible solutions that might help to overcome this problem that can be derived from the empirical findings of the questionnaire study.

The questionnaire revealed that only few referees took over this post because friends or relatives told them about this activity (average score 2.5 on the five-stepped Likert Scale). This result shows that this honorary post is little propagated in the referees` social surrounding. Grunig/Grunig/Dozier (2002) identified public relations as a useful tool for organizations to improve the communication with its stakeholders and minimize conflicts.[79] This approach can also be transferred to the referees as they form an organization that finds itself in the network of sports stakeholders. Therefore, it is first of all advisable to increase the effort in public relations in order to increase the public awareness of this function.

---

[79] Cf. Grunig/Grunig/Dozier (2002, p. 2)

So far, this effort was limited to a homepage that leaves room for improvement and scattered articles in the local newspapers.[80] What is missing is a structured, consistent PR and advertising strategy. This would comprise a complete revision of the homepage in a first step. Currently, the homepage lacks optical attractiveness and the contents are not updated due to missing personal resources. However, it is advisable to commission a relaunch of the website by a specialist. The costs (approximately EUR 150.00) have already been budgeted and approved.[81] Another way of doing PR is to approach the local newspapers. Beech and Chadwick (2007) point out that the media helps to increase the public awareness of sports.[82] Indeed, this has been done in the past, but not on a regular basis. It should be the aim to be constantly present in the newspaper. This can be achieved by a weekly column or regular articles that are concerned with latest news such as promotions of referees, events, new referees and other current topics. Again, the basis for this kind of PR exists and simply has to be extended.

What has not been in place yet, but appears to be a promising tool to recruit new referees, is to create an appealing information flyer. The aim should be to illustrate the referee activity with all its positive aspects, but also not neglecting the obligations that come along with it in order to convey a complete and honest impression. The consequence then can be that the aspirants who want to become a referee due to the information in the flyer are intrinsically motivated as they have a thorough understanding of what they can expect from being a referee. These approaches of creating transparency are also known as 'Signaling' strategy in the framework of the Principal-Agent Theory. However, it shall be remarked that normally the Agent has to apply these measures. In the referees` case, this is done by the Principal (the KSA). The contents of these PR measures shall be oriented on the motives the current referee uttered in regard to their driving factors to become a referee. The results from the empirical analysis show that the most significant reasons for choosing this honorary post refer to individual and 'Psychological Needs'.

---

[80] The online representation of the referee in Guetersloh can be assessed under the following web address: http://www.flvw-k34.de/fileadmin/file_uploads/schiedsrichter/index.html
[81] The costs of this planned relaunch will approximately amount to EUR 150.00 and will be covered by the sports committee of Guetersloh
[82] Cf. Beech/Chadwick (2007, p. 11)

The highest average scores relate to the motive of taking over responsibility on the match field (average score 4.3) and of feeling good and relieved after good matches (average score 4.1). For this reason, the aim of the PR measures shall be to stress the psychological benefits of this activity. In order to appeal as well to young as to old referees, further advantages shall not be neglected in this form of advertising. On the one hand, the younger the referees are, the more likely they are referee because they see a good chance of promotion. On the other hand, the older the referees are, the higher they value the reason of staying in shape. The importance of those PR activities is also supported by Taylor/Doherty/McGraw (2007) who figure out an increased use of the peoples` social network to recruit staff.[83] This tendency becomes even more striking when considering that the referees do not pursue this activity because they were approached by their clubs (average score 2.0). Thus, there seem to be further sources the interest originates in. Those shall be addressed with this PR strategy accordingly.

6.2 Missing Quality of Referee Aspirants

It was stated that the lack of referees is a challenging task which shall be accomplished by attracting new aspirants with PR measures. However, with the increasing quantity, the number of inappropriate aspirants increases disproportionally at the same time. This is, because the clubs announce the candidates. At the same time, the managing-committee cannot evaluate the appropriateness of the aspirants prior to the beginning of the qualification.

The Principal-Agent Theory refers to this situation as the problem of 'Hidden Characteristics'. As a classical example of such a relationship, the example of the manager (principal) and an applicant (agent) for a job in the company shall be consulted. Presuming that the principal does not know the agent, he cannot perfectly assess the agent`s abilities and appropriateness ex ante. Even if the applicant conveys a good impression, the principal might make a wrong decision by hiring the applicant. The underlying problem is that the principal cannot observe the agent`s performance ex ante, namely before offering him a contract. This danger is conferred to as 'Adverse Selection'.

---

[83] Cf. Taylor/Doherty/McGraw (2007, p. 69)

Coming back to the referees` case the initial problem is that the clubs` interests do not correspond with the KSA`s intention to develop good and motivated referees (quality > quantity) as the clubs primarily try to fulfill the required number of referees (quantity only) so that fines resulting from the "3-Stufen-Plan" (see Fig. 11) can be avoided. Although many aspirants are not suitable for the position of a referee, they take part in the qualification program and the KSA is not allowed to reject inappropriate candidates. Only if they are repeatedly absent during the qualification program, the managing-committee can dismiss them. This is even a worse situation than the 'classical' case of 'Adverse Selection'. In reference to the manager of a company, it becomes obvious that he has the chance to reject candidates that he considers as inappropriate. As the KSA does not have this authority, the danger of 'hiring' and qualifying unsuitable aspirants increases significantly. This problem leads to agency costs in form of extra work for the KSA due to short-dated returns of matches or a lack of availability, insufficient participation in both the monthly meeting and the annual test and consequently to a bad performance during the matches. In the end, those issues may also result in the referee`s dismissal. The Principal-Agent Theory proposes screening, signaling, and self selection strategies in order to avoid the problem of 'Hidden Characteristics'.[84] Signaling strategies are pursued by the agent in order to openly demonstrate his or her own abilities.[85] This can be reached by handing in certificates, reports or further confirmation of participation. Basically, this solution can find application in the referees` case.

They can signal their motivation and appropriateness by being present on every qualification day, by achieving good results in the tests and by demonstrating attention and interest. However, there is no urgent need for signaling the abilities as the candidates will be accepted anyways, regardless of whether they are well qualified or not. The most common reason to apply this strategy is to demonstrate a strong intrinsic motivation and the will to be promoted as soon as possible at a very early stage. Still, only very few referees follow this strategy and thus, there is no significant potential for the KSA to recognize unsuitable aspirants in advance. Regarding the missing quantity of referees, the approach of structuring the PR measures was already mentioned.

---

[84] Cf. Miller (2008, pp. 349-367)
[85] Cf. Wickham (2006)

With the aim of increasing the number of candidates, the chance of recruiting appropriate aspirants also increases. As the Principal-Agent Theory names signaling strategies by the agent as a means to decrease the 'Information Asymmetry' in the constellation, the PR efforts of the KSA again can be considered as an 'atypical' form of signaling, because it is conducted by the principal.[86] This is not surprising as the managing-committee is in need of new agents and therefore has to present itself as an attractive option.

Another approach that is proposed by the theory is a 'Self (adverse) Selection' mechanism. In this case, the principal offers the agent various contracts from which he can choose. Montias/Ben-Ner/Neuberger (1994) remark that the principal can learn more about the agent`s intention depending on the choice he makes.[87] Assuming that there is a contract with a fixed salary and a contract with a lower fixed salary and a variable bonus structures for a good quality and quantity of the outcome, it can be assumed that the agent that chooses the latter will make a higher effort than the agent that chooses a fixed salary. This is, because the agent who chooses the fixed salary does not have any incentive to perform extraordinarily. This solution can be neglected in the referees` case. The aspirants do not have the chance to negotiate any parameters of their activity as a referee as they do not sign any contract. Furthermore, they are treated equally and their remuneration is fixed (see Fig. 13). Overall, only the last-named approach can be applied in this case. The managing-committee appears as the principal in this constellation and has a major interest in recruiting motivated referees who are reliable. Thus, the prospective aspirants could be screened by the KSA before they start the qualification. More concretely, the KSA could set up a profile of every referee. This fact sheet might contain data such as age, motives and aims in regard to the referee activity and functions of the aspirant in the club: With this information, a first impression of the candidate can be gained and the information asymmetry between both parties is reduced. In order to deepen this first impression, the members of the KSA should have individual conversations with the prospective referees. This creates a more personal atmosphere and the aspirant`s ambitions, his expectations regarding the activity as a referee, and his commitment can be figured out.

---

[86] Cf. Picot/Reichwald/Wigand (2008, p. 49)
[87] Cf. Montias/Ben-Ner/Neuberger (1994, pp. 48-49)

Another way to screen the referee`s appropriateness is to offer the joint watching of a football match in the district which is refereed by a colleague. The intentions are manifold. First of all, this serves as an opportunity to increase the community spirit, but also to evaluate which of the candidates appear at all and thus show motivation. Again, the information asymmetry can be reduced accordingly. The KSA can furthermore use this event as a signaling means by showing that the participation in obligatory events is expected from the referees. Thirdly, practical qualification work can be conducted as it has become obvious that new referees have trouble in applying the theoretical knowledge during their matches correctly. In detail, evaluating the referee`s performance according to the assessment sheet (see Fig. 14 and 15) will help the aspirants to understand, what they have to take into account and how to react in the matches, they will referee as soon as they passed the final exam. Due to the decreased 'Information Asymmetry', both means serve as a screening tool and convey a first thorough impression of the aspirant and his accuracy for the referee activity. Based on the fact sheet and the personal conversation, the KSA then can decide whether to accept the aspirant for the qualification program or not. As this has not been possible so far, the KSA needs to be provided with this competence by the sports committee of the district. Due to the good cooperation and the obvious need for changes, this concern most probably will be accepted. However, it has to be remarked that this right to reject aspirants has also drawbacks in terms of the quantity of new referees. Furthermore, introducing a deposit for the education of every aspirant can be helpful to increase the referees` quality. More concretely, the clubs could be obliged to pay a caution for every candidate they announce. In case the candidates do not act properly during the education or do not attend regularly, the caution then would not be refunded. However, it shall be remarked that this caution should not exceed 50 Euros as this might deter the clubs from naming candidates at all. The intention simply shall be to create a certain barrier in order to make the club think more about which candidates they assign. The missing quality of referee aspirants is only one of many problems in the work of the KSA. Learning more about the aspirants before actually educating them seems to be very promising. Furthermore, introducing a mandatory deposit might lead to an 'forced alignment' of the clubs` and KSA`s view, namely that quality is more important than quantity.

It was addressed, how the aspirants` quality can be improved. In a next step, the problems concerning the active referees will be regarded.

6.3 Unreliability of active Referees

Besides the inappropriateness of many aspirants and the lack of referees, further problems have to be regarded. After having passed the final examination, the new referees have to obey the existing rules and regulations. However, in many cases this does not happen as many of them do not show up during the monthly meeting and reject matches or take over only few games. According to the Principal-Agent Theory, this result can be ascribed to the aspirants` 'Hidden Characteristics'.[88] It was already described that the managing-committee does not have any influence on the choice of aspirants and cannot reject unsuitable candidates. Moreover, the KSA does not have an impact on how possible solutions can look like. Still, it may happen that referees turn out to be unmotivated and unreliable after the examination. The Principal-Agent Theory does not directly refer to this kind of problem, but proposes a solution that might help to increase the new referees' compliance. Installing bureaucratic control can be a useful means to achieve this. It can be learned from the regular employment market how this might be done.

This is, because many companies set up contracts with an employment probation period.[89] This term reduces the risk of hiring a candidate that does not fulfill the requirements although he or she conveyed a good impression during the application process. The same mechanism could also be installed in the presented case. During the half-season probation (equivalent to four months) the new referee can prove that he or she is willing and motivated. Consequently, the managing-committee can evaluate whether or not to continue the cooperation after this period of time. The main criteria for this decision can be the regular participation in the monthly meetings and reliable takeover of matches. This mechanism can be applied for the new referees, but cannot be adapted for the experienced ones.

---

[88] Cf. Campbell (1995, p. 8)
[89] The German labour law specifies this probation period for a professional training with one month to four months (§ 20 Berufsbildungsgesetz (BBiG). This guideline seems also appropriate for the time after the referee qualification

When having passed the exam, the aspirants directly proceed to the regular referee activity without being explicitly informed about their duties and rights regarding this activity. A basic assumption of the Principal-Agent Theory is that the relationship is stipulated.

In reference to Beale/Bishop/Furmston (2008), contract law basically regulates the agreements between two or more parties.[90]

According to Blum (2007), a contract can be defined by four crucial elements.

> *1. An Oral or written agreement between at least two persons*
> *2. A relationship that is based on an exchange*
> *3. One or more promises*
> *4. Enforceability[91]*

Considering the case, it becomes obvious that such a contract is not in place although the relationship between the managing-committee and the referees is based on an exchange (of the referee activity itself). What is missing is an explicit oral or written agreement that specifies the duties and obligations of the parties, the exact promise, leading to enforceability. In order to create a more binding and obligatory basis for the cooperation, all referees shall sign a 'contract' that specifies the rights and duties.

The existing referee constitution can not only be used in regard to the duties and rights before and after the match, but also for the jurisdiction against referees. What needs to be added are the concrete directives in regard to the monthly meeting, the match confirmation and rejection of assignments and the participation in the annual test. This 'contract' shall not exceed two pages to make sure that it is understandable and really supported by the referees. It shall be considered as the referees' declaration and will to comply with the contents. In order to create a binding character, the referees shall sign this declaration. This agreement is a formal device that specifies the referees duties and rights and shall serve as a means to increase the awareness of the parameters that come along with the activity of being a referee.

---

[90] Cf. Beale/Bishop/Furmston (2008, p. 3)
[91] Cf. Blum (2007, p. 2)

Similarly to their new colleagues, the experienced referees do not participate frequently in the monthly meetings and the annual test. When the questionnaire was filled out by the referees during the monthly meetings in September, 133 forms should have been returned in order to reach a census of all referees in Guetersloh. However, only 62 questionnaires were completed.

As every referee who attended the monthly meeting in September received a form it can be seen that the participation is (mostly) below 50% of the total number. The participation in the annual test is even worse. Although three different dates are offered, less than 50 referees attend this obligatory event on average.[92] In order to identify the reasons for this low participation, the referees were asked what their opinion in regard to these events is. The results shall help to detect potential for improvement and thereby to increase the participation. The study shows that the monthly meetings are perceived positively as for example the atmosphere during the monthly meetings was rated high (average score 3.9). This impression is supported by the finding that the referees perceive the form of presentation as comprehensive (average score 4.1). It is also important to notice that the older the referees are the more the referees think that the length of the theoretical part is appropriate and interesting. The reasons for participating in the monthly meetings therefore go along with the positive perception of this obligatory event. Furthermore, the referees state that their participation is not reasoned in their will not to be punished by being assigned to 'unattractive matches'.

The reason for this is that they are much more interested in the theoretical qualification. Again, the scores for interesting contents and the chance to learn more about the rules increase as the referees` age increases. Although the opinion regarding the monthly meetings is positive, the number of participants is not satisfactory. The questionnaire reveals that many referees attend the monthly meeting because it is obligatory (average score 4.1). Basing on the questionnaire, there can be no further significant reasons be identified. The same phenomenon is valid for the annual test. The most significant reason for attending the test again is its obligatory character (average score 4.2).

---

[92] This number is based on the attendance in the last six years

Moreover, the referees have an intrinsic motivation to figure out their own abilities (average score 3.9) and to show that they feel certain in regard to the theoretical rules (average score 3.8). As can be seen, the reasons for the participation in the annual test are similar to the reasons for attending the monthly meetings. The referees` valuation of this statement leads to the idea of distracting the referees from the mandatory aspect of the monthly meeting and the annual test.

This can inter alia be reached by integrating the referees in the design of the monthly meetings. As they do not have any influence so far, it may be advisable to allot special topics of the theoretical work to the referees. There are various advantages of this approach. First of all, the KSA is unburdened. However, this shall not be the crucial reason. If a presentation or a report is presented by one or more referees, they will prepare this as good as possible in order not to be embarrassed in front of the group. This means that they might learn more by preparing a topic on their own than to simply listen to a presentation by the KSA members.

Furthermore, presentations by a colleague represent a variety and this might lead to higher attention and thus to a better understanding of the contents.According to Fülöp/Ross/Kuscer/Pucko (2007), another tool to foster the motivation can be the introduction of a competition as the people might show more dedication to the task.[93] In order to guarantee an objective valuation of the referees` performance during the season, a scheme with different parameters shall be introduced.

A possible 'scorecard' can look as follows.

---

[93] Cf. Fülöp/Ross/Kuscer/Pucko (2007, pp. 238-239)

Parametre	Points
Participation in the monthly meeting	3 per attendance
Participation in the annual test (Theory)	
0 mistakes	20
0,5-3 mistakes	17
3,5-5 mistakes	14
5,5-8 mistakes	11
8,5-10 mistakes	8
> 10 mistakes	5
Participation in the annual test (Running)	
Passed	15
Not passed	5
Matches refereed	2 per match
Takeover of an extra match	5 per match
(short term, due to a cancellation of a colleague)	
Extraordinary behavior	8
(presentations, report, shop steward)	

Fig. 17: Referee Competition: Scorecard

This scorecard requires an exact recording of the points. As the participation in the monthly meetings, the annual test including the results and the matches refereed are recorded anyways, this does not mean extra work for the KSA. According to McClelland (1987), it is essential to offer lucrative incentives to foster the motivation in this regard in order to prevent the agents (referees) from acting exclusively on their own behalf.[94] Furthermore, it is advisable to award a prize to more than one winner in order to make the chance of winning more probable. Ten prizes seem to be appropriate considering that there are 133 active referees. This shall lead to an increased effort of all referees and excludes a subjective evaluation of the competition. However, there shall be different prizes for the first ten places to foster a competition until the last match day of the season. At the end of a season, all winners can be honored with an article in the local newspapers and an online article on the homepage.

---

[94] Cf. McClelland (1987, p. 229)

As already pointed out, the PR effort of the managing-committee shall be increased. Thus, this article represents another pillar of the aforementioned PR. Possible incentives are listed below. However, there is of course room for other solutions.

Place	Prize	Costs
1	Two tickets for the Executive lounge of a North Rhine-Westphalian team in the German 'Bundesliga' or for a match of the German National Team.	0 Euros (the tickets can be obtained from the FLVW)
2	Tracksuit including a T-Shirt	About 70 Euros
3	Voucher for a dinner in a restaurant in Guetersloh	40 Euros
4	Two tickets for a visit of a brewery	About 40 Euros
5	T-Shirt and Shorts in the official FLVW design	About 40 Euros
6	Two tickets for "Das Aktuelle Sportstudio"	About 30 Euros
7	Two tickets for the Gerry Weber Open	About 30 Euros
8	Free drinks during the monthly meetings (one season)	About 30 Euros
9	One free drink during each monthly meeting (one season)	About 10 Euros
10	Set of hygiene products	About 10 Euros

Fig. 18: Possible Prizes for the Referee Competition

Surely, the prizes have to be financed. However, the sum of circa 300 Euros can be taken from the budget the KSA receives from the council of the district and is not a crucial problem. The monthly meeting is primarily intended to qualify the referees for the matches they are assigned to. The aim is to reduce the issues resulting from 'Hidden Action'. This is another problem resulting from 'Information Asymmetry' in a Principal-Agent constellation. In contrast to 'Hidden Characteristics' the problems resulting from 'Hidden Action' become obvious after having made the contract in this relationship.[95] The basic problem lies in the hidden performance of the agent, because according to Cataldo (2003) the principal mostly cannot completely monitor the agent`s action with economically reasonable means.[96] This leaves the latter a certain scope of action. This phenomenon can also be transferred to the case. The referees` 'Hidden Action' during their matches causes various problems. First of all, potential breaches of the rules by the referee cannot be thoroughly observed and thus are nearly inevitable. This might lead to undesired trials at the court of arbitration. Moreover, the referees are alone in most cases. This makes it easier for other parties involved to leverage the referee and thus make him or her feel uncomfortable and insecure.

---

[95] Cf. Cahuc/Zylberberg (2004, p. 323)
[96] Cf. Cataldo (2003, p. 10)

Especially young and inexperienced referees suffer from this and they might give up their activity as a consequence. In the same context, the young referees could also be advised how to treat player, coaches, or other officials from the clubs who do not behave properly. Over and over again, the inexperienced referees report that they had trouble with exactly this issue. As soon as the players and other participants recognize the referee`s insecurity, they try to make use of it. In many cases, this endeavor ends up in unforeseen problems.

Picot/Reichwald/Wigand (2008) propose control schemes as a possible approach to reduce the 'Information Asymmetry' in this context.[97] This solution goes along with the PAT and is most often reached by applying monitoring devices such as cameras that tape the agents and their work effort, but also time-recording systems. Especially monitoring seems to be an effective instrument in the case in Guetersloh as thereby the performance can be critically examined and the chance of breaches of rule and excessive pressure on the referee can at least be stemmed. For that reason, the referees` attitude towards coaching mechanisms was evaluated. The empirical analysis revealed that there is a positive tendency towards the effectiveness of coaching by colleagues. The score for the statement saying that colleagues might give useful tips and advice for one`s own matches was rated above average (3.6). Moreover, the referees stated that they would not feel uncomfortable if they were monitored by the KSA (average score 2.0) and even perceive this as a motivating factor (average score 3.6). Therefore, the basic requirements for an effective monitoring system are given.

However, the managing-committee can only imperfectly monitor the referees during their matches due to missing financial and personal resources. Still, the KSA values this task very high and tries to monitor as many colleagues as possible. Due to the given constraints a selection has to be made. Consequently, the young and new referees are monitored and coached preferably during their first matches in order to give them useful advice and increase their self-confidence. In exceptional cases, such as repeated complaints by clubs regarding the referee, more experienced colleagues are also monitored to figure out if the complaints are justified.

---

[97] Cf. Picot/Reichwald/Wigand (2008, p. 48)

Besides this specific monitoring, further solutions to improve the performances during the match must be found. The monthly meetings have been reduced to theoretical education which refers to the rules and regulations only. Due to the missing monitoring devices, the referees have to be prepared for the situations that might occur during their matches. A practical qualification therefore is necessary as well. Instead of a regular monthly meeting the referees should also be coached how to react in stress situations such as after awarding a penalty, a dismissal with the second yellow or the red card, massive complaints and misbehavior of players, coaches, or other officials. These situations can be created with the help of role plays, the referees act in. One of them always finds himself in the situation of the referee and is asked to react to the best of his ability. After each situation, the respective referee then is asked how he felt and why he reacted the way he did. Subsequently, the other participants have the chance to discuss the scene and the referee`s performance. In so doing, all referees can participate actively and learn from each other. Moreover, the KSA gets an impression of where weak points are and can also directly influence the referees` behavior in his own interest.

As it was pointed out before, the participation in the monthly meeting currently is insufficient. Thus, the idea of training the referees currently cannot be pursued satisfactory. Again, the need for increasing the participation in a first step becomes obvious. The ideas for reaching this have already been introduced. According to Campbell (2006), incentives are a basic means to foster the agent`s general performance.[98] Concerning the case, the referees could be rewarded for good performances during the matches. However, this solution is not feasible for the case. There is no opportunity to receive an objective and competent evaluation of the referees` behavior as there is no independent institution that could assess the performance. A pure monetary reward for the referees` performance is not possible due to the given constraints. Their remuneration strictly follows the division they are assigned to (see Fig. 13) and cannot be influenced in any form. Thus, a performance related bonus payment is not possible.

---

[98] Cf. Campbell (2006, p. 6)

Besides the 'Hidden Action', the Principal-Agent Theory also refers to the problem of 'Hidden Information'.[99] In this case the principal can monitor the agent and his activities, but lacks the knowledge to judge the quality. Transferring this to the referees means that the KSA would not have the expertise to review the referees' performance on the match field. Indeed, every member of the KSA was or still is active in divisions on FLVW level. Especially the person in charge of the assignments has expert knowledge and thus is even aware of animosities of clubs towards referees and vice versa. Moreover, critical matches therefore are regularly refereed by experienced or high-class colleagues in order to avoid problems.

6.4 Bribery and Game Manipulation

The last problem area resulting from Principal-Agent relationship is the agent's 'Hidden Intention'. Even if the KSA could monitor every match in the district, the referees' intention would remain latent. The KSA puts itself in dependence on the referees by qualifying and assigning them to matches. This is, because the motive of maintaining the competition by assigning an official referee to each match can only be reached with a sufficient quantity and quality of referees.

What this exactly means becomes obvious when considering the problems regarding game manipulation and bribery. Not only is the current manipulation affair in the professional football in Europe object to 'Hidden Intention' of players and referees, but also in non-professional football. In the past, more and more irregularities in the matches were discovered. Especially in the lower divisions that face little presence in the newspapers, games are manipulated. Clubs that find themselves in the relegation or promotion battle offer their opponents incentives in form of money or beer for a deliberate loss at the end of a season. This trend surely may not be stopped by the interference of referees. However, what concerns the KSA most is that the referees play an increasingly important role in this constellation. The questionnaire study revealed that 18% of 30 referees have been offered money by club representatives for conscious decisions to the benefit of the respective team. The maximum amount offered is 300 Euros.

---

[99] Cf. Lane/Ersson (2000, p. 48)

The actual number of referees who have been approached in this regard might even be higher even though the questionnaire was filled out anonymously. As the referees cannot be perfectly monitored, other ways to limit the potential of game manipulation must be found. The analysis of the referees` motives shows that their reasons for choosing this activity often refer to personality issues. The referees obviously like to take over responsibility (average score 4.2) and feel happy and relieved after matches (average score 4.1). Additionally, there is no significant score for the statement: "I am a referee to earn money" (average score 2.6). Concluding from these empirical results, it can be said that the referees basically do not seem to be open to bribery and manipulation. However, this tendency still is prevailing. Effective counter measures therefore have to appeal to issues that are of importance for the referee. Thus it seems to be promising to set up a 'Code of Conduct' for the referees. The intention of this document shall be to appeal to the referees` morale and sportsmanship. The contract therefore shall contain promises referring to the honor and morale of referees and their responsibility for a fair competition. The referees shall additionally sign this contract to create a binding, 'legal' character. This contract is to be understood as a tool to foster the common culture among the referees.

Concluding, it can be said that the problem of bribery can only hardly be solved due to the given constraints. A formal and binding document might help to appeal to the referees` morale and thus to decrease their openness to game manipulation. Nonetheless, this issue is not only of interest for the KSA, but also for the entire football. After having analyzed the various problems explicitly, motivational aspects and the role of punishment will now be addressed as separate topics.

6.5 Motivation

So far, the prevalent problems were elaborated on with the help of the Principal-Agent Theory. The focus will now be set on the contribution of the motivational theories that were introduced. As the activity represents an honorary office, it seems to be promising to learn more about the referees` motivation.

This view is also supported by Farrell/Johnston/Twynam (1998) who figured out that sport organizations must understand their employees' motivation to let them perform efficiently.[100] In order to do so, Maslow's Needs Hierarchy will be regarded in a first step. Victor Vroom's Expectancy Theory will then be used subsequently to find further approaches for the case solution.

6.5.1 Application of the Needs Hierarchy

Maslow systematically illustrates the hierarchy of human needs that range from basic needs such as shelter and salary to 'Self-Actualization Needs' such as a challenging job.[101] Applying this theoretical approach to the referees might help to learn more about their basic motivation to take over this position. In doing so, the Needs Hierarchy shall be regarded with a bottom-up approach. According to Maslow (1943), the most basic needs are of physiological nature.[102] These comprise money and shelter, for example. In the presented case, this level of needs is not the decisive factor to become a referee. As German citizens, the arbitrators are part of the welfare state and neither suffer from extreme poverty nor from homelessness. Although it may be remarked that they receive a monetary reward for their activity, this remuneration does not represent a significant factor to ensure financial stability, but rather a small income source. The second level refers to the safety of oneself, the family and other important objects.[103] Again, the referee activity cannot be reasoned by this needs level as it does not provide any form of safety. In contrast, being a referee is directly linked with conflicts during the matches and thus does not satisfy 'Safety Needs'. 'Love Needs' as the third layer of needs cannot be the decisive factor for a person to become a referee for the same reason. As already pointed out, the referee function rather leads to the task of facing conflicts with players and officials of the teams. The next step in the Needs Hierarchy is referred to as 'Esteem Needs'.[104] When fulfilling 'Esteem Needs', an individual wants to be unique with self-respect and to gain the esteem from other individuals. Exactly this seems to be the most common reason to become a referee. By taking over this task, the individuals are responsible for the adequate adherence to the rules.

---

[100] Cf. Farrell/Johnston/Twynam (1998, pp. 288-289)
[101] Cf. Maslow (1943, pp. 370-396)
[102] Cf. Ibid.
[103] Cf. Ibid.
[104] Cf. Ibid.

This is directly linked with reaching a certain status in the local sports scene. Especially for the young referees, promotion can be an important reason to become a referee and thus to achieve personal aims. All these aspects have an immediate impact on the person`s esteem as a consequence. According to Maslow, the most abstract need is to self-actualize oneself.[105] This can be reached by experiencing and realizing all inner potentials. Considering the referee activity, it is questionable if this activity suffices to satisfy the needs of self-actualization. It may be argued that this 'hobby' cannot help to self-actualize oneself. However, being a referee at the same time means to cope with criticism, stress and other challenging situations. The empirical analysis shows that many referees see an opportunity for personal growth in this honorary task.

Concluding, it can be said that the motives for being a referee typically are not to be found in the basic needs. With reference to Maslow, 'Physiological', 'Safety' and 'Love Needs' are no crucial factors in the decision process to become a referee. 'Esteem Needs' in a first place, but also 'Self-Actualization Needs' represent the determinants to be a referee to a much greater degree. This is, because the aforementioned needs are fulfilled to a satisfactory extent. Surely, the individual aspiration might differ among the referees.[106] However, what they have in common is that the basic needs are fulfilled due to the given circumstances in Germany and the social system that the citizens are in. Consequently, the people strive to fulfill further, more abstract needs. This apparently can be reached with the referee activity.

With this knowledge, many means to foster motivation can be disregarded as they might not be effective. This means that for example increasing the remuneration will be attractive for the referees, but might not have a positive substantial effect on the motivation level as this need ('Physiological'). However, considering Maslow`s Needs Hierarchy can also lead to possible solutions to increase the arbitrators` motivation. Several approaches to reduce the current problems in the KSA`s work have already been elaborated basing on the Principal-Agent Theory. It was pointed out that introducing a 'Code of Conduct' can be a helpful means to decrease the problems resulting from bribery and game manipulation by appealing to the referees` values and morale.

---

[105] Cf. Maslow (1943, pp. 370-396)
[106] Cf. Negandhi/Savara (1989, p. 93)

Furthermore, including the referees in the work of the KSA also seems promising and supportive to foster the referees` esteem as this conveys the impression that they are needed and valuable for the community. All those measures appeal to 'Esteem Needs'. This shows that the solutions derived from the PAT go well along with the findings from Maslow's Needs Hierarchy. This, in turn, additionally backs up the proposed approaches

Concluding, it is important to notice that this theoretical approach presents a rather holistic view on human needs. Its focus therefore is to systematically illustrate the different human needs instead of delivering tools to solve specific problems. Nonetheless, it can be said that Maslow`s Needs Hierarchy is relevant for the referees` case as it backs up the findings from the PAT and the empirical analysis.

6.5.2 Application of the Expectancy Theory

In contrast to Maslow who structures the different forms of human needs, Victor Vroom aims at examining how various factors influence the decision of an individual. According to Vroom, the level of motivation is the product of the 'Expectancy', the 'Instrumentality' and the 'Valence' of a certain action.[107] When analyzing the referees` behavior, it has to be remarked that their actions cannot be determined by one single motive. It shall therefore be investigated how the decision in regard to the participation in the monthly meeting and the annual test, but also the attempted bribery is influenced with respect to the Expectancy Theory.

It has already been pointed out that the insufficient participation in the monthly meeting results in various problems the KSA is faced with. The decision process for or against attending the meeting shall be analyzed with watching a movie on TV ('Television') as an exemplary alternative option. The 'Expectancy' of both options shall be regarded in a first step. In doing so, the probability of a good performance when choosing a certain effort has to be determined. This 'Expectancy' is relatively low in the referees` case. The intention of improving the referees` performance is not fully reached although important theoretical and practical advice is given during the monthly meetings. This is mainly due to two reasons.

---

[107] Cf. Vroom (1964, p.20)

First of all, the high average number of mistakes in the theoretical test at the end of every season shows that the referees` knowledge of the rules is unsatisfactory. Furthermore, the scattered monitoring of single referees reveals that the quality of the practical performance during the matches is also not sufficient. Contrarily, the alternative of watching a movie does not imply a certain 'Expectancy' level in terms of Vroom`s Expectancy Theory as choosing this alternative does not have an influence on the performance in any sense.

The second element of Vroom`s theory is the 'Instrumentality' of a certain action. Sloof/Van Praag (2005) state that 'Instrumentality' answers the question of how probably the good work will lead to the desired outcome.[108] In reference to attending the meeting, this can mean that participating in it most shall lead to the assignment to interesting matches or the promotion to a higher division on district level at the end of a season. Indeed, the attendance of the monthly meeting is the major determinant for the KSA`s choice, which referees are promoted or relegated at the end of a season. The other factors are the participation in the annual test and the practical performance during the matches. In comparison, watching TV instead of attending the monthly meeting cannot be directly linked to work. Still, it has to be remarked that the desired outcome most probably will be reached. The most common motives for watching TV are to be entertained or to relax. As the viewers can freely decide, which program to watch, these aims normally are reached. Thus, the 'Instrumentality' of this option - according to Vroom – is also high.

The third determinant of the Expectancy Theory is the 'Valence' of a certain action. 'Valence' describes the importance of the outcome for an individual.[109] The empirical analysis shows that the older the referees are, the less they took over this activity because the wanted to be promoted. Additionally, it has been proved that the referees` motives generally are based on 'Psychological Needs' such as the will to take over responsibility. As the decision whether to attend the monthly meeting and the annual test or not is not directly linked to this motive, the 'Valence' is low. In our example, the 'Valence' of watching TV instead is high, as it is most probably connected with a positive feeling.

---

[108] Cf. Sloof/Van Praag (2005, p. 7)
[109] Cf. Maslow (1964, p. 20)

Basing on this learning, the KSA will have to focus on reducing the attractiveness of not participating in the monthly meeting and the annual test. According to the Expectancy Theory, increasing the 'Valence' of attending the obligatory meetings is in this case the most efficient measure. It has already been pointed out how this can work. Including the referees in the design of the meetings can lead to an increased 'Valence' as they will feel accepted and needed. This might develop a feeling of belongingness and thus an increased value for the referees. Furthermore, introducing a competition (see Fig. 17) also is a motivating factor to show up during the meetings. The importance of alternative activities consequently is reduced.

Another problem in the KSA`s work with the referees is the increasing number of detected game manipulations. Examining this behavior with the help of the Expectancy Theory leads to the learning that there is no 'Expectancy' in this case. The referee can consciously make decisions in favor of one team and has no interest in his own 'good' performance. The probability that his effort will lead to the desired outcome (receiving money from the club) consequently is 100%, because the referee has massive influence on the result of the match. However, the 'Valence' has the most important impact on the referee`s decision to be open to bribery or not. As the outcome is of monetary nature, it can be directly quantified. Thus, the sum of money offered must be sufficient for the referee to take the risk of being detected and act immorally. Increasing the probability of being convicted consequently leads to a decreased 'Valence' of manipulating a match.

It has already been pointed out that an increased monitoring effort is not feasible due to financial and personal restrictions. Even if these restrictions were not given, monitoring matches would not automatically lead to the detection of bribery as the referees` decisions have to be made immediately and always are subjective. The conscious preference of one team can only hardly be proved accordingly. Another approach to deter the referees from bribery again is represented by the introduction of a referees` 'Code of Conduct' which was already introduced. As this idea was already brought up before, it shall not be explained further. The intention again is to appeal to the referees` sportsmanship with a binding character, created by the personal signature of them.

Concluding, the Expectancy Theory by Victor Vroom can generally be applied to the case. It becomes obvious that increasing the 'Valence' of the desired action, respectively reducing the 'Valence' of its alternative option is the most effective approach as the 'Expectancy' and 'Instrumentality' in this case do not have a major impact on the referees` choice. What has been neglected in this context is the effectiveness of punishment as a negative enforcement of certain actions. This influencing means shall be regarded in the following.

6.6   The Effectiveness of Punishment

Besides the contribution of motivational aspects for the solution of the case, the effectiveness of punishing misbehavior shall also be contemplated separately. The questions of where and how the penalization has to be set up to serve as a useful tool will be answered in this context. In a first step, Becker`s Deterrence Hypothesis is taken into consideration to pay attention to possible findings from the scientific theory on punishment. The focus shall also be set on the referees` attitude towards punishment, because the findings from the theory are not taken as the only decisive factor for the evaluation. In order to install efficient forms of prosecuting misdemeanors, it is important to know how the referees perceive the current mechanisms. Remembering that the empirical analysis on punishment bases on a two-stepped Likert Scale the scores have to be interpreted differently from the other parts of the analysis.[110]

6.6.1 Application of the Deterrence Hypothesis

Becker`s Deterrence Hypothesis shall be taken as a theoretical tool in order to evaluate the current forms of punishment. In the following, the equation and its components will be transferred to the referees` case. The aim will be to evaluate why the current forms of punishments do not have the desired effects. According to Becker (1968), an 'optimal' decision in regard to the crime level means reducing the damage resulting from the crime itself, chasing the delinquent and the costs for applying the punishment.[111]

---

[110] The questionnaire study was based on a three-stepped Likert Scale with the answers "Yes" (Code 1), "No" (Code 2) and "I don't know" (Code 3). The third option was disregarded in the evaluation in order to receive only answers showing a tendency. As a result of this exclusion, the number of answers is reduced to 35.
[111] Cf. Becker (1968, p. 207)

The expected gain from committing a crime can be calculated as shown below.[112]

$$EU_i = (1 - p_i) * U_i (Y_i) + p_i * U_i (Y_i - f_i)$$

With:

U_i: Utility function (gain);

Y_i: Value of the illegal booty (can be monetary and psychological);

p_i: The probability of being convicted;

f_i: The monetary equivalent of the punishment;

6.6.1.1   Value of the illegal Booty

Looking at Becker`s Deterrence Hypothesis, it can be figured out that reducing the value of the illegal booty (Y_i) leads to a decreased gain from committing a crime (EU_i) as an increased Y_i leads to an increased result of both addends of the equation.

Assuming that

$p_i,$ = 1% (0.01),

Y_i = 50 Euros (money offered by the club for the game manipulation), and

f_i = 80 Euros (refund of the booty plus a fine of 30 Euros for committing the crime)

the gain function looks as follows:

$$EU_i = (1 - 0.01) * U_i (50) + 0.01 * U_i (50 - 80)$$

$$\Leftrightarrow EU_i = (0.99) * U_i (50) + 0.01 * U_i (-30)$$

$$\Leftrightarrow EU_i = 49.5 * U_i (50) - 0.03 * U_i$$

$$\Leftrightarrow EU_i = 49.47 * U_i$$

---

[112] Cf. Becker/Landes (1974)

Increasing the value of the booty to 200 Euros while holding all other factor constant results in the following gain function:

$$EU_i = (1 - 0.01) * U_i (200) + 0.01 * U_i (200 - 230)$$

$$\Leftrightarrow EU_i = (0.99) * U_i (200) + 0.01 * U_i (-30)$$

$$\Leftrightarrow EU_i = 198 * U_i – 0.03 * U_i$$

$$\Leftrightarrow EU_i = 197.97 * U_i$$

It becomes obvious that the higher the value of the booty is, the higher the gain from committing the crime is. Even if the fine was dramatically higher in the latter case, the gain still would be higher than in the case with a EUR 50 booty. The value of the illegal booty for the referee can either be a monetary reward resulting from game manipulation or bribery or presents from the clubs. Y_i also comprises all advantages that cannot be directly quantified. One way to make committing a crime less attractive is to reduce the value of the outcome. Firstly, there might be a significant monetary advantage from a malicious game manipulation. The referees are offered money for consciously making decisions in favor of the respective team in most cases.

As these actions can normally not be detected, there is no chance for the KSA to influence the value of the booty. Transferring the Deterrence Hypothesis to the unexcused absence during the monthly meeting and/or the annual test leads to the learning that the value of the booty cannot be precisely quantified. This is, because the absence does not result in a direct monetary advantage for the referees. The only obvious positive consequence of this behavior is that the referees can spend the time with doing more pleasant activities. This cannot be influenced by the referees as every person can freely decide how to spend one`s spare time. What can be seen is that influencing the value of the booty is not possible in most cases. Thus, there have to be other ways to reduce the attractiveness of the booty and the value of EU_i.

6.6.1.2 The Probability of being convicted

Another factor that affects the attractiveness of committing a crime is the probability of being convicted for the misdemeanor.[113] By increasing p_i, the result of $(1-p_i)$ decreases and thus, $(1 - p_i) * U_i (Y_i)$ decreases accordingly. However, it must be remarked that with an increased p_i, the result of the addend $p_i * U_i (Y_i - f_i)$ necessarily increases at the same time. Still, the result of EU_i decreases with a higher probability of being convicted (p_i). This is, because in the second addend, the monetary equivalent of the punishment (f_i) is deducted from the value of the illegal booty. It therefore becomes obvious that the impact of p_i on the result is higher in the first addend than in the second. Thus, a low p_i automatically leads to higher gain EU_i than a high probability of conviction.

Regarding the insufficient participation in the monthly meeting and the annual test, the gain for the referees is exactly $U_i (Y_i - f_i)$. This is, because the probability is $= 1$ (100%) as every missing referee is noticed and punished in case of an unexcused absence. For $p_i=1$, the expected gain function is as follows: $EU_i = (1 - 1) * U_i (Y_i) + 1 * U_i (Y_i - f_i)$. The result of the first addend is $=0$ which means that it can be dropped out of the term. The term $1 * U_i (Y_i - f_i)$ remains.

Thus, the gain from committing a crime with a 100% probability is the difference between the value of the booty (this is the spare time resulting from not participating in the obligatory events) and the monetary equivalent of the punishment. This is a fine of five Euros for not attending the annual test. A fine for being absent during the annual test is currently not in place. According to Becker`s economic view on crime, the referees will be absent without excuse as long as they value the spare time or the effort for excusing oneself higher than five Euros. Another situation is to be found in case of game manipulation and bribery. As already pointed out, the KSA does not have the financial and personnel resources to monitor every match in Guetersloh.

---

[113] Cf. Becker (1968, p. 207)

It now shall be analyzed how probable the conviction must be. Given that the value of the booty (money offered for the manipulation) is 50 Euros and the monetary equivalent of the punishment is the refund of the booty plus a fine of 30 Euros, the expected gain from manipulating games is calculated as follows:

$$EU_i = (1 - p_i) * U_i (50) + p_i * U_i (50 - 80)$$

$$\Leftrightarrow 0 = 50 - 50 * p_i + 50 * p_i - 80 * p_i$$

$$\Leftrightarrow 80 * p_i = 50$$

$$\Leftrightarrow p_i = 0.625$$

Basing on the assumptions made, the referees would manipulate the match as long as the probability of being detected is below 62.5 %. However, it has to be remarked that this consideration refers to economic factors only and disregards psychological, social and further influences. This finding leads to the learning that the KSA would have to extend the monitoring efforts. This however is not feasible due to the given financial and personal constraints. In fact, only about 1 % of the matches can be monitored under the given circumstances. Moreover, the major ratio of monitored games is refereed by young colleagues who per se are less open to bribery at the beginning of their career. As can be seen, the means to decrease the level of crime by fostering the probability of being convicted the KSA are limited. Furthermore, monitoring matches does not automatically mean that game manipulations can be detected. For that reason, the KSA has to find other approaches to reduce the attractiveness of opposing to the effective rules and clauses.

6.6.1.3 Monetary Equivalent of the Punishment

Besides the probability of being convicted, Becker also considers the monetary equivalent of the punishment in case of detection as a decisive factor regarding the decision for or against committing a crime.[114] According to the Deterrence Hypothesis, the gain from committing a crime decreases with an increased monetary value of the punishment. In order to prove this, the gain EU_i from committing a crime will be calculated basing on two different values for f_i. All other factors shall be held constant in order to avoid unwanted deviations.

---

[114] Cf. Becker (1968, p. 207)

The probability of being convicted (p_i) again shall be 1%. The value of the illegal booty (Y_i) is 50 Euros and the monetary equivalent of the punishment in the first case shall be 100 Euros. This leads to the following gain function.

$$EU_i = (1 - 0.01) * U_i (50) + 0.01 * U_i (50 - 100)$$

$$\Leftrightarrow 49.5 - 0.5$$

$$\Leftrightarrow 49$$

As can be seen, the gain EU_i in this case is relatively high. In order to elaborate the influence of a higher monetary equivalent of the punishment, f_i shall now be 1.000 Euros. This gives the following equation.

$$EU_i = (1 - 0.01) * U_i (50) + 0.01 * U_i (50 - 1.000)$$

$$\Leftrightarrow 49.5 - 9.5$$

$$\Leftrightarrow 40$$

Still, the gain from committing the crime is positive. This is due to the low probability of being convicted. However, it becomes obvious, that the gain in the constellation with a higher monetary equivalent of the fine is significantly lower. This proves that with an increasing f_i the gain (EU_i) decreases.

6.6.1.4 The Costs of Law Enforcement

According to Becker, the state (in the case the KSA) has to decide whether or not to pursue the delinquent (the referees). This however shall always be economically rational. Considering the relation between the probability (p_i) and severity of the fine (f_i) on the one hand and the costs of law enforcement on the other hand (see Fig. 2) it can be seen that not every constellation of p_i and f_i can be reached with the given cost function. As the financial resources are strictly limited the KSA has to apply monitoring devices that guarantee an acceptable level of crime while the costs for ensuring this do not exceed a reasonable economic level. Exactly this happens in the referees` case.

The persons who monitor matches are active or passive referees and receive a pay of five Euros per match as an additional compensation to the way they travel.[115] As the financial resources of the KSA are limited, a thorough monitoring system cannot be installed. Furthermore, the personal resources are limited, because there are only a few persons who are willing to do this monitoring job. Even if these prerequisites were given, detecting game manipulations still would be hardly possible. In most cases, the agreement on manipulating a match is made before the respective game. This can either happen via telephone or early before the matches. The chance of detecting such an agreement therefore is dramatically low and does not justify massive expenses on trying to reveal game manipulations in the referees` case.

6.6.1.5 Other Forms of Punishment

As can be seen, the hypothesis provides various approaches to decrease the level of crime. However, the theory concentrates on economic aspects of crimes exclusively and lacks the consideration of further influencing factors such as social norms, psychological aspects and personal traits. We shall now have a look on how the referees perceive the approach of punishing misbehavior in order not to neglect their opinion. It was figured out that the probability of being convicted and the severity of the fine are two decisive factors for the decision to commit a crime or not. When considering the scientific work of Becker it may not be disregarded that this approach focuses on the economic effects of crimes. Consequently, further important aspects in the decision making process are ignored by Becker.

When analyzing the case of referees in non-professional football, the economic features of the decision to comply with the existing rules or not to obey them do not suffice. It was already pointed out that psychological motives play a relevant role for the position of a referee. The questionnaire study shows that the most significant reasons for being a referee are the will to take over responsibility and the positive feeling after matches that were refereed without problems. Thus, the personal traits will also impact the referees` decision to disregard the existing duties such as attending the monthly meeting and the annual test.

---

[115] The current compensation is 0.30 Euros per travelled kilometre (to the match and back home).

In this context, the introduction of a 'Code of Conduct' again appears as a tool that may deter the referees from committing a crime by appealing to their morale and their social norms. This idea may reduce the level of unwanted behavior by the referees. Still, the issue of not attending the monthly meeting and the annual test will not be solved satisfactory. The monetary fines may have a slight reducing effect, but do not seem to be the appropriate tool. Going beyond Becker's Deterrence Hypothesis, the monetary equivalent of the punishment (the fine in the referees' case) is only one possible solution to punish misbehavior. Considering the referees' psychological and 'Esteem Needs', a non-monetary form of punishment may be even more effective. The most common way is to relegate the referees in case of insufficient participation in the monthly meeting and absence during the annual test. However, when considering a relegation of referees, one basic problem comes into play that the KSA has to cope with. This is not only the insufficient number of referee aspirants, but also the number of active referees. In order to assign a referee to every match in all divisions, there have to be enough candidates for every league on district level. As can be seen in Figure 8 there are 65 referees in the "Kreisliga B" and Kreisliga C". These referees are normally assigned to matches in the respective senior leagues, but also to matches in the A- and B-Junior divisions.

This means that in total, there are about 60 matches every weekend to be assigned with referees from the "Kreisliga B" and "Kreisliga C". However, not all of the referees are available at the weekend. This is due to various reasons such as injuries, illness or private appointments. In many cases the referees additionally exercise other honorary posts such as being a coach or also actively play in a team themselves. This leads to problems in the assignment process as simply not all referees are available at the weekends. As a consequence, even if the KSA wants to apply the relegation as a form of punishment, this is not possible in many cases as either the referees already are active in the lowest division or a relegation would lead to a lack of referees in a certain division. As the referees are also aware of this fact, this form of punishment currently cannot be effective. Referring back to the referees' motives it was also figured out that psychological and personal reasons play an important role. Thus, relegating a referee might be more effective than applying fines for misdemeanors. Given that the recruitment process is optimized and more aspirants are appropriate candidates, the number of referees will increase.

This tendency then would make a punishment in form of relegation possible. However, this has to be considered as a long-term goal due to the given circumstances.

6.6.2 Empirical Evidence

Punishments have to be realizable and accepted by the delinquents in order to be effective at all. The empirical study consequently also aimed at investigating the means to foster compliance. The referees were asked if the fine for the unexcused absence during the monthly meetings was justified in a first step.[116] This basic requirement obviously is met as the average score of 1.2 represents a clear tendency of agreement. This shows that the referees basically admit that not attending the monthly meetings is a misdemeanor which shall be punished. The referees also consider the current fine for this delinquency as appropriate (average score 1.2). However, it may not be disregarded that the referees most probably would not say that the fine is too low, because admitting this cannot be advantageous for them. An increased fine strictly would lead to a worse situation for the referees and thus, this result shall not be valued too highly. Accordingly, the referees do not think that the fine should be higher to be effective (average score 1.7). In order to evaluate how effective the current forms of punishment really are, the referees were asked if the fines deter them from misbehavior. The average score (1.7) in this case shows that the fines do not have the desired effect. This tendency is supported by the finding that the introduction of a fine for not participating in the annual test would rather not have a deterrent effect (average score 1.7).

Furthermore, a fine for the late rejection of matches would not lead to a more punctual rejection of an assigned match. In reference to Becker`s Deterrence Hypothesis, the severity of the punishment plays an important role in the decision making process of a potential delinquent even though according to Roberts (2003), its impact is lower than the one of the conviction probability.[117] A basic precondition for the effectiveness of punishment is that the delinquent is directly connected to it.

---

[116] Note that the fine for an unexcused absence during the monthly meeting is five Euros
[117] Cf. Roberts (2003, p. 315)

However, this is not necessarily the case for the referees in Guetersloh as the empirical analysis shows that the majority of the referees do not have to refund the fines. Instead, their clubs take over the payment. Thus, the deterrent effect cannot be reached as the there is only little personal liability for the individuals.

7 Critical Valuation

This work is aimed at assessing the elements of the scientific approach in regard to their contribution for the solution of the case. On the one hand, relevant theories were figured out and applied to the case. On the other hand, an empirical study was conducted to learn more about the referees, their motivation and the effectiveness of punishment. The applied theories and the empirical analysis will be critically evaluated in regard to their relevance and contribution concerning the case solution in the following section.

7.1 Assessment of the applied Theories

All applied theories will be regarded in terms of their contribution to the case solution in this section. The Principal-Agent Theory as main theoretical element will be examined in a first step. Secondly, Abraham Maslow`s Needs Hierarchy will be judged accordingly. In the following, the Expectancy Theory will be regarded. The critical valuation of the theories then will close with the assessment of Becker`s Deterrence Hypothesis.

7.1.1 The Principal-Agent Theory

As the case analysis is primarily based on the relationship between the Principal and the Agent, the contribution of this theory shall be evaluated in a first step. The Agency-Theory refers to constellations in which one person acts on behalf of another. The underlying problem of such a relationship is the asymmetric information between both parties. A common example (among others) for such a relationship is the case of a manager or employee who acts on behalf of a company owner or another stakeholder.[118] The duties and rights of both parties are written down in a formal contract. However, not all elements of the interaction can be perfectly embraced in this document. These circumstances can also be found in the interaction between the managing-committee and the referees in Guetersloh.

---

[118] Cf. Grundtvig/Furubotn/Richter (2000, p. 149)

With the assignment of referees to matches, the KSA mandates them to act on their behalf. In doing so, the KSA has to face the problems that arise in such a relationship accordingly. It was pointed out that the problems in a Principal-Agent relationship ('Adverse Selection', 'Hidden Action' and 'Hidden Information', but also 'Hidden Intention') can also be detected in the case presented. The analysis of the referees` situation leads to the learning that the PAT is a very useful tool to address the existing problems. This is, because the Theory proposes various solution mechanisms to overcome the problems. As those are rather holistic, an application to the case is only possible if the approaches are narrowed down. It has been found out that many solution mechanisms (signaling and screening strategies) for the problems in a Principal-Agent relationship are of practical relevance for the case and allow for a realistic application. What becomes obvious in regard to the differences between the theory and the case is that the PAT is based on a contract, whereas the interaction between the referees and the KSA is not based on such a legal agreement. As a consequence, their binding character is not sufficiently obeyed by the arbitrators. On the one hand, this difference is a possible solution for the case at the same time as the introduction of such a document might increase the referees` awareness and willingness to follow their obligations. On the other hand, it has to be remarked that being a referee on this level is a hobby and the introduction of a contract that restricts the referees` behavior might also have a deterrent effect in regard to the continuation of this activity. As can be seen, the Principal-Agent Theory is not only applicable to constellations in business environment, but has already been extended to relationships in other contexts such as the mutual interaction between a teacher and the pupils or the role of a doctor who treats patients.

What has been neglected to a large extent in scientific literature is the application of the theory to sports-related issues as in the case presented. This thesis therefore might be a starting point for more scientific work in this segment as Principal-Agent relationship can be detected easily in the sports network. Examining the interaction of a coach with the players or the club management in professional football with regard to the Agency-Theory, for instance, might be another interesting project.

7.1.2 The Needs Hierarchy

Maslow developed the Needs Hierarchy in 1954 with the intention to systematically illustrate the different levels of desires on a universal level. When evaluating its contribution from today`s point of view, Heylighen (1992) criticized the lack of scientificity and the integrated concept.[119] Schott and Maslow himself (1992) furthermore critically assessed the concept`s overall validity.[120] Wahba/Bridwell (1976) additionally questioned the contribution of research evidence.[121] In contrast to the Principal-Agent Theory, Abraham Maslow`s Needs Hierarchy focuses on human needs exclusively. The Needs Hierarchy consequently cannot be viewed as a theory in a pure sense as it is limited to a simple visualization. Thus, its contribution to the case solution is rather low, because it does not provide any solution mechanisms or advice for problems that are related to human needs. Regardless of this fact, the illustration provided input for the case solution as it supports the empirical findings.

The analysis of the referees` motivation showed that their motives are mostly related to 'Psychological' and 'Esteem Needs'. Exactly this finding is supported by the results of applying the Needs Hierarchy to the case presented. Examining each level separately shows that the referees` basic needs, such as 'Physiological', 'Safety', 'Love' and 'Belongingness Needs' are generally fulfilled. Taking into account the referees` general situation in Guetersloh, the question why referees exercise this activity is answered by the third and fourth level of needs which are 'Psychological' and 'Self-Actualization Needs'. In this case, the theoretical approach is additionally supported by the empirical findings from the questionnaire that was filled out by the referees during one of their monthly meetings.

7.1.3 The Expectancy Theory

Victor Vroom`s Expectancy Theory is intended to explain the human motivation for a certain action. However, it does not offer practical approaches to influence human motivation.[122]

---

[119] Cf. Heylighen (1992, p. 40)
[120] Cf. Schott/Maslow (1992, p. 109)
[121] Cf. Wahba/Bridwell (1976, p. 212)
[122] Cf. Li (2006, p. 259)

The theory consists of the pillars 'Expectancy', 'Instrumentality' and 'Valence'.[123] Similarly to the Needs Hierarchy, this theoretical approach is universally applicable. What makes it different from Maslow`s approach is that practical recommendations for the KSA can be drawn from it. The theory was applied to two different problems of the KSA`s work. Firstly, this is the insufficient participation in the monthly meeting and secondly the increasing number of game manipulations.

It was shown that the most important factor of the referees` motivation is the 'Valence' of their actions. The basic problem is that there are manifold alternatives to attending the monthly meeting whose importance is rated higher. As the KSA does not have any chance to decrease the importance of alternative options such as watching TV, the 'Valence' of attending the meeting has to be increased. This can be reached by an incentive scheme for positive behavior (see Fig. 18) or the referees` integration into the design of these meetings. In reference to the problem of game manipulation, the KSA might reach a decreased level by appealing to the referees` morale. Concluding, it can be said that the Expectancy Theory allows for more concrete recommendations than Maslow`s Needs Hierarchy. However, it has to be considered as a supporting theory and not as the major determinant for the case solution.

So far, the focus of the critical valuation was mainly set on the referees` motivation. What has to be considered as well is the influence of punishment in this context. In doing so Gary S. Becker`s Deterrence Hypothesis was applied. The influence of this theory shall be elaborated in a next step.

---

[123] Cf. Vroom (1964, pp. 14-16, 128)

7.1.4 The Deterrence Hypothesis

Becker's Deterrence Hypothesis delivers interesting approaches to the question of whether and how punishments can be successful, namely in which cases they can be an appropriate measure to reduce the level of crime. According to the theory, the severity of the punishment and the probability of being convicted are the major influences on the level of crime.[124] Transferring this consideration to the football referees' case results in the learning that due to the given monetary and personal constraints, an increased probability of being convicted cannot be reached when acting economically rational. However, the severity of the punishment which in the umpires' case mostly is a fine can be influenced more easily.

When critically analyzing the hypothesis, it has to be remarked that Becker's theory was developed in 1968 and therefore cannot obey current developments. Additionally, the hypothesis follows exclusively an economic approach to this topic. Becker focused on the optimal relation between costs of law enforcement such as catching and convicting the delinquent and the social gain the conviction implies for the society. This view does not suffice for the problem solution in this work. This is exactly where most of the criticism of the hypothesis is uttered. The criticism mainly focuses on the lack of long-sightedness of Becker's Deterrence Hypothesis. It is often claimed that there are further aspects to be taken into consideration when analyzing the effectiveness of crime. Reiss (1980) claims that the social situation of a delinquent also has to be taken into consideration within the framework of deterrence.[125] According to Dnes (2000), unemployment and poverty can for example affect the crime level of a society as well.[126] Furthermore, many authors remark that not the fine itself leads to the abandonment of the illegal behavior but rather the moral and social values which are linked to a fine.

Fielding/Clarke/Witt (2000) argue that unemployment (social influence) and a mental disease (biological factor) also may impact the decision of an individual to commit a crime or not to do so.[127] This has also been elaborated in the empirical analysis.

---

[124] Cf. Becker (1968, p. 207)
[125] Cf. Reiss (1980)
[126] Cf. Dnes (2000, p. 71)
[127] Cf. Fielding/Clarke/Witt (2000, p. 71)

The main influence of the referees` behavior is related to 'Psychological Needs' and motives. Thus, when analyzing the influence of fines, the economic aspect does not suffice to solve the problem satisfactory in this case. Therefore, the contribution of the Deterrence Hypothesis in regard to solution strategies is rather low as it does not take the circumstances of the respective delinquency into account. However, the application of the theory shows that it is also valid for the referees` context. Concluding, one can say that Becker´s Deterrence Hypothesis focuses on the economic aspects of fines and lacks the fore-sightedness which the development in the past forty years (since its origin in 1968) demands. Adaptations due to changes in both the economic and social segment were not incorporated and as a result, Becker´s Deterrence Hypothesis lacks the appropriateness to address the problems from today`s point of view.

Basically, it has to be remarked that the contributions of the theories to the case solution differ. According to the basic intention of this work, the Principal-Agent Theory represents the major theoretical approach as it can be very well applied to the case. Consequently, most of the recommendations from theoretical point of view were extracted from the PAT. The Expectancy Theory by Victor Vroom also delivers some proposals for optimizing the work of the KSA with the referees. Maslow`s Needs Hierarchy is only of little relevance, because no solutions can be identified to solve the issues. Becker`s Deterrence Hypothesis was considered separately from the aforementioned theories as its focus lies on the effectiveness of punishment. Despite the fact that the Deterrence Hypothesis lacks the contemplation of current developments, it focuses on the economic aspects of crime and delinquency exclusively. This finding at the same time is the major criticism in terms of the theory`s contribution for this work. As was figured out, the referees` motivation cannot be assessed sufficiently with an economic approach.

So far, the theories were assessed in a first step. The other scientific approach to the case solution was the realization of an empirical analysis to receive further information on the referees´ situation and motives and attitudes towards their activity. The contribution of this study will be examined in the following.

7.2 Assessment of the Empirical Study

The application of aforementioned theories was the first of two pillars that were used to solve the case. In order to elaborate a solution strategy that is efficient and effective, the referees were also directly included. This was realized with a questionnaire that was filled out by the referees during a monthly meeting. The questionnaire was written in German and filled out anonymously after having introduced the set-up and the intention to the referees in a first step in order to receive reliable and useful results. Initial questions were directly answered to avoid misunderstandings. Additionally, support was offered while the referees worked on the questionnaire. The fact that no help was needed conveyed the impression that the questionnaire was set up clearly. Furthermore, only two out of sixty-two questionnaires could not be evaluated. This additionally shows that the questionnaire was understandable. The only critical aspect with regard to the empirical analysis may be seen in the sort of referees that answered it. As already pointed out, one basic problem of the KSA`s work is the insufficient participation in the monthly meeting. Consequently, the problematic group of referees consists of the ones that are absent during these meetings. Therefore, a certain number of referees may not have been reached with the questionnaire in case they were not present when the study was conducted. However, this issue has been taken into consideration by choosing a monthly meeting with many participants. Additionally, the study was split up in order to reach as many referees of the respective groups (youth, district level and FLVW level).

62 questionnaires were distributed during the monthly meeting of the different groups, of which all were returned. Two of them could not be evaluated as the personal data section was not filled out. This did not allow for a valid interpretation of the result as for example the referee`s age and the division he or she is active in remained unknown. These questionnaires therefore were not included in the analysis of the results. Moreover, only the significant results of the regressions (with a $P>|t|$ of ≤ 0.05) were considered. The contemplation of motives and statements was limited to average scores that deviated strongly from the average. Thus, only results with an average score of ≤ 2.2 or ≥ 3.8 (the average in the five-stepped Likert Scale is 3.0) were regarded in order to receive meaningful findings.

Concluding, it can be said that the empirical analysis resulted in interesting findings which delivered practical approaches to the displayed problems. It becomes obvious that integrating the referees and their attitude towards their hobby in the case solution is essential. This is, because the solution mechanisms directly affect their situation. As the intention of this work is to elaborate realizable measures to improve the referees` situation in Guetersloh, the questionnaire turned out to be the most relevant and important scientific pillar.

After having critically evaluated the contribution of the applied theories and the questionnaire study, an overall conclusion of the work and an outlook will be given in the following.

8 Conclusion and Outlook

This work aimed at answering the question of how the problems in the interaction of the KSA with the referees in Guetersloh can be solved with particular regard to motivation and punishment. In order to do so, the Principal-Agent Theory served as the major theoretical basis. In order to examine motivational issues more thoroughly, Maslow`s Needs Hierarchy and Victor Vroom`s Expectancy Theory were taken into consideration. Furthermore, Becker`s Deterrence Hypothesis was contemplated in regard to the role of punishment in the case presented. Besides the theories applied, a questionnaire was designed to back up the findings from the theory with practical recommendations. When considering the KSA`s situation, it has to be acknowledged that the basic problem of their work is the insufficient number of referees. This constellation is advantageous for the referees, because they do not have to show extraordinary determination as they are needed anyways. For the same reason drastic forms of punishment such as the dismissal of a referee can only hardly be applied in order not to jeopardize the maintenance of the competition. Consequently, it will be essential to foster the recruitment of new referees in future to let the performance and behavior be decisive for or against the referee`s continuance. Once the number has increased, the KSA can apply punishment as a regulatory means for an increased compliance. Considering the Principal-Agent Theory, the lack of a contractual agreement that regulates the rights and duties of a referee is another major problem.

Thus, the introduction of such a formal, binding document is a promising means that might increase the referees` obedience to their duties. Furthermore, the introduction of a 'Code of Conduct' can help to remind the referees of their morale and thus to reduce their openness to bribery and game manipulation. Due to the given circumstances, the insufficient participation in the monthly meeting and the annual test therefore should be antagonized with a positive enforcement of compliant behavior. This can for example happen by introducing a competition that refers to the participation in the monthly meeting, the annual test, but also extraordinary behavior. The empirical analysis furthermore reveals that the referees` perception of the monthly meetings is positive. This shows that the design of the meeting is not the decisive factor for not attending this obligatory event.

To sum up, it can be said that the effectiveness of punishment is strictly limited due to the insufficient number of referees in the current situation. Only if the number of referees can be increased in the long-term, this means can be applied to solve the problems. The most promising approach therefore is to positively enforce the referees` compliance and to appeal to their values. Regardless of these findings, it has to be acknowledged that the situation the KSA is confronted with is also transferable to other honorary posts. In the past years, the number of persons in honorary posts has dramatically decreased due to various reasons. It will therefore be the major task of the KSA to increase the number of referees significantly. If this can be reached, the current problems may be solved in the long-run.

Bibliography

AKERLOF, G. A. (1970): "The Market for 'Lemons': Quality Uncertainty and the Market Mechanism," *The Quarterly Journal of Economics*, 1970, Vol. 84, issue 3, p. 488-500

ANDERHUB, V., GAECHTER, S. AND KOENIGSTEIN, M. (2002): *"Contracting and Fair Play in a Simple Principal-Agent Experiment,"* Humboldt University Berlin, p. 2

ATCHISON, T. J. AND HILL, W. W. (1978): *"Management today – Managing Work in Organizations,"* p. 188

BEALE, H. G., BISHOP, W. D. AND FURMSTON, M. P. (2008): *"Contract: Cases & Materials,"* 5th Edition, Oxford University Press, p. 3

BECKER, G. S. (1968): "Crime and Punishment: An Economic Approach," *Journal of Political Economy*, 76 (2), pp. 169-217

BECKER, G. S. (1974): "Crime and Punishment: An Economic Approach," in: BECKER, G. S. AND LANDES, W. M. (EDTS.) (1974): *"Essays in the Economics of Crime and Punishment,"* National Bureau of Economic Research, p. 2

BEECH, J. G. AND CHADWICK, S. (2007): *"The Marketing of Sport,"* Pearson Education Limited, p. 11

BÉNABOU, R. AND TIROLE, J. (2003): "Intrinsic and Extrinsic Motivation," *Review of Economic Studies,* 70, pp. 489–520

BLUM, B. A. (2007): *"Contracts: Explanations and Examples,"* 4th Edition, p. 2

BLUMSTEIN, A. ET AL. (EDTS.): *"Deterrence and Incapacitation: Estimating the Effects of Criminal Sanctions on Crime Rates,"* National Academy of Sciences, Washington, DC, p. 140-173 AND G. HAWKINS (1973): *"Deterrence: The Legal Threat in Crime Control,"* University of Chicago Press, Chicago

BRIER, S. S. AND FIENBERG, S. E. (1980): *"Recent Econometric Modeling of Crime and Punishment. Support for the Deterrence Hypothesis?"* Sage Publications, pp. 150-153

CAHUC, P. ANG ZYLBERBERG, A. (2004): *"Labor Economics,"* The Massachusetts Institute of Technology Press, p. 323

CAMPBELL, D. E. (1995): *"Motivation and the Economics of Information,"* Cambridge University Press, p. 7

CAMPBELL, D. E. (2006): *"Incentives: Motivation and the Economics of Information,"* 2nd Edition, Cambridge University Press, p. 6

CATALDO, A. J. (2003): *"Information Asymmetry: A Unifying Concept for Financial and Managerial Accounting Theories,"* Elsevier B. V., p. 10

COASE, R. H. (1937): "The Nature of the Firm," *Economica*, New Series, Vol. 4, No. 16

COON, D. AND MITTERER, J. O. (2008): *"Introduction to Psychology: Gateways to Mind and Behavior,"* p. 339

DECI, E. L. AND RYAN, R. M. (2000): "The 'What' and Why' of Goal Pursuits: Human Needs and the Self-Determination of Behaviour," *Psychological Inquiry*, 11, pp. 227-268

DNES, A. W. (2000): "The Economics of Crime," in: FIELDING, N. G., CLARKE, A. AND R. WITT, R. (EDTS.) (2000): *"The Economic Dimensions of Crime,"* Macmillan, p. 71

EISENHARDT, K. M. (1989): "Agency Theory. An Assessment and Review," *Academy of Management Review,* 1989, 1, pp. 57–74

ERLEI, M., LESCHKE, M. AND SAUERLAND, D. (2007): *"Neue Institutionenökonomik,"* 2. Aufl., Stuttgart, p. 13

FARRELL, J. M., JOHNSTON, M. E. AND TWYNAM, G. D. (1998): "Volunteer Motivation, Satisfaction, and Management at an Elite Sporting Competition," *Journal of Sport Management [JSM]*, 12(4), pp. 288-289

FIELDING, N., CLARKE, N. AND WITT, R. (2000): *"The Economic Dimensions of Crime,"* MacMillan Press Ltd., p. 71

FOSS, P. (1995): *"Economic Approaches to Organizations and Institutions,"* p. 188

FREY, B. S. AND JEGEN, R. (2000): "Motivation Crowding Theory: A Survey of Empirical Evidence," Revised Version, *Journal of Economic Surveys*, 2001, 15 (5), pp. 589-611

FREY, B. S. (2009): *"Punishment – and beyond,"* University of Zurich, ETH-Zurich and CREMA – Center for Research in Economics, Management and the Arts, Switzerland (this version May 26, 2009), p. 1

FUNK, P. (2001): *"Kriminalitätsbekämpfung",* Mohr Siebeck, p. 25.

FURUBOTN, E. G. AND PEJOVICH, S. (1972): "Property Rights and Economic Theory: A Survey of Recent Literature," *Journal of Economic Literature*, Vol. 10, 1972, pp. 1137-1162

FURUBOTN, E. G. AND RICHTER, R. (2000): *"Institutions and Economic Theory: The Contribution of the New Institutional Economics,"* Michigan, p. 149

FÜLÖP, M., ROSS, A., KUSCER, M. P. AND PUCKO, C. R. (2007): "Competition and Cooperation in Schools: An English, Hungarian and Slovenian Comparison," in: SALILI, F. AND HOOSAIN, R. (EDTS.) (2007): *"Culture, Motivation and Learning – A Multicultural Perspective,"* Information Age Publishing Inc., pp. 238-239

GINTIS, H. (2000): *"Game Theory Evolving: A Problem-Centered Introduction to Modeling Strategic Interaction,"* Princeton University Press, p. 332

GOLASH, D. (2005): *"The Case against Punishment: Retribution, Crime Prevention, and the Law,"* New York University Press, p. 1

GRUNIG, L. A., GRUNIG, J. E. AND DOZIER, D. M. (2002): *"Excellent Public Relations and Effective Organizations: A Study of Communication Management in Three Countries,"* Lawrence Erlbaum Associates, p. 2

HEYLIGHEN, F. (1992): "A Cognitive Systematic Reconstruction of Maslow's Theory of Self-Actualization," *Behavioral Science*, 37, pp. 39-58

HUESMANN, L. R. AND PODOLSKI, C. L. (2003): "Punishment: A Psychological Perspective," in: MCCONVILLE, S. (EDT.) (2003): *"The Use of Punishment,"* p. 59

JENSEN, M. C. AND MECKLING, W. H. (1976): "Theory of the Firm: Managerial Behavior, Agency Costs and Ownership Structure," *Journal of Financial Economics*, 3 (1976), pp. 305-360

KESER, C. AND WILLINGER, M. (2002): *"Theories of Behavior in Principal-Agent Relationships with Hidden Action,"* p. 2

LANE, J.-E. AND ERSSON, S. O. (2000): *"The New Institutional Politics: Performance and Outcomes,"* Routledge, p. 48

LATHAM, G. P. (2007): *"Work Motivation: History, Theory, Research, and Practice,"* Sage Publications, p. 4

LEIPOLD, H. (1975): „Vertragstheorie und Gerechtigkeit", in: GUTMANN, G. AND SCHUELLER, A. (EDTS.) (1989): *„Ethik und Ordnungsfragen der Wirtschaft,"* Baden-Baden, pp. 357-385

LI, L. (2006): *"Human Motivation in the Work Organization: Theories and Implications,"* New Asia College, Academic Annual, XIX, pp. 253-263

MASLOW, A. H. (1943): "A Theory of Human Motivation," *Psychological Review,* Vol. 50, 1943, pp. 370-396

MASSIE, J. L. (1979): *"Essentials of Management,"* 3rd Edition, pp. 144-145

MCCLELLAND, D. C.: *"Human Motivation,"* Press Syndicate of the University of Cambridge, p. 229

MICELI, T. J. (2004): *"The Economic Approach to Law,"* Stanford University Press, p. 290

MILLER, G. J. (2005): "Solutions to Principal-Agent Problems in Firms," in: MÉNARD, C. AND SHIRLEY, M. M. (EDTS.) (2008): *"Handbook of New Institutional Economics,"* Springer, pp. 349-367

MINER, J. B. (2005): *"Organizational Behaviour – Essential Theories of Motivation and Leadership,"* p. 109

MONTIAS, M., BEN-NER, A. AND NEUBERGER, E. (1994): *"Comparative Economics,"* Harwood Academic Publishers GmbH, pp. 48-49

MOOK, D. G. (1987): *"Motivation: The Organization of Action,"* p. 4

MORGAN, G. (1943): *"Images of Organization,"* 2nd Edition, p. 36

NEGANDHI, A. R. AND SAVARA, A. (1989): *"International Strategic Management,"* p. 37

O`NEIL, H. F AND DRILLINGS, M. (1994): *"Motivation: Theory and Research,"* p. 83

PICOT, A. AND DIETL, H. (1990): „Transaktionskostentheorie," *„Wirtschaftswissenschaftliches Studium,"* 19. Jg., Heft 4, pp. 178-184

PICOT, A., DIETL, H. AND FRANCK, E. (1999): *"Organisation – Eine ökonomische Perspektive,"* 2. Aufl., Stuttgart, pp. 85-94

PICOT, A., REICHWALD, R. AND WIGAND, R. (2008): *"Information, Organization and Management,"* Springer, pp. 48-49

PRATT, J. W. AND ZECKHAUSER, R. J. (1985): *"Principals and Agents: The Structure of Business,"* Harvard Business School Press, Boston, Massachusetts

QUIGGIN, J. AND CHAMBERS, R. G. (2003): "Bargaining Power and Efficiency in Principal-Agent Relationships," *Risk & Uncertainty Program Working Paper,* Paper Number 1/R03, p. 1

REISS, A. JR. (1980): "Understanding Changes in Crime Rates," in: FIENBERG, S. AND REISS, A. JR. (EDTS.) (1980): *"Indicators of Crime and Criminal Justice: Quantitative Studies,"* Department of Justice Statistics, Washington, D.C.

ROBERTS, A. R. (2003): *"Critical Issues in Crime and Justice,"* 2nd Edition, Sage Publications, p. 315

ROSEN, S. (1988): "Transaction Costs and Internal Labor Markets," in: WILLIAMSON, O. E. Williamson AND WINTER, S. G. (EDTS.) (1993): *"The Nature of the Firms – Origins, Evolution and Development,"* pp. 83-84

SCHOTT R. AND MASLOW, A. H. (1992): "Humanistic Psychology, and Organization Leadership: A Jungian Perspective," *Journal of Humanistic Psychology,* 32(1), p. 109

SCHUHMANN, J. (1987): „Die Unternehmung als ökonomische Institution," *„Das Wirtschaftsstudium,"* 16. Jg., pp. 212-218

SLOOF, R. AND VAN PRAAG, C. M. (2005): "Performance Measurement, Expectancy and Agency Theory: An Experimental Study," *Scholar Working Papers Series,* WP 52/05, p. 7

TAYLOR, T., DOHERTY, A. AND MCGRAW, P. (2007): *"Managing People in Sport Organizations: A Strategic Human Resource Management Perspective,"* Butterworth-Heinemann, p. 69

TIROLE, J. (1988): *"The Theory of Industrial Organization,"* The Massachusetts Institute of Technology Press, Cambridge, p. 35

VROOM, V. H. (1964): *"Work and Motivation,"* Wiley, pp. 14-15, 20, 128

WAHBA, M. AND BRIDWELL, L. (1976): "Maslow Reconsidered: A Review of Research on the Need Hierarchy Theory," *Organizational Behavior and Human Performance*, 15, pp. 212-240

WEINBERG, R. S. AND GOULD, D. (2007): *"Foundations of Sport and Exercise Psychology,"* p. 139

WICKHAM, P. A. (2006): *"Strategic Entrepreneurship,"* 4th Edition, p. 145

WILLIAMSON, O. E.: *"The Economic Institutions of Capitalism,"* New York: Free Press, 1985

ZIMRING, F. E. AND HAWKINS, G. (1973): *"Deterrence: The Legal Threat in Crime Control,"* University of Chicago Press, Chicago

ZIMRING, F. E. (1978): "Policy Experiments in General Deterrence: 1970-1975," in: BLUMSTEIN, A., COHEN, J. AND NAGIN, D., (EDS.): *"Deterrence and Incapacitation: Estimating the Effects of Criminal Sanctions on Crime Rates,"* National Academy of Sciences, Washington, DC, p. 140-173

ZOU, L. (1989): *"Essays in Principal-Agent Theory,"* Louvain-la-Neuve: CIACO, p. 3

Online Sources

Deutscher Fußball-Bund:
http://www.dfb.de/index.php?id=11292 (Access 08/21/2009)

Fußball- und Leichtathletik-Verband Westfalen:
http://www.flvw.de/fussball/senioren/3-stufen-plan.html (Access 08/31/2009)
http://www.flvw.de/fussball/senioren.html (Access 08/31/2009)
http://www.flvw.de/fussball/jugend/spielbetrieb/durchfuehrungsbestimmungen.html (Access 08/31/2009)

Landesbank NRW:
www.landesdatenbank.nrw.de (Access: 08/25/2009)

Appendix

The Questionnaire for the Referees in Guetersloh

Fakultät für Psychologie und Sportwissenschaft

Abteilung Sportwissenschaft

Wintersemester 2009/2010

Fragebogen zum Thema „Motivation von Schiedsrichtern im Amateurfußball"

Liebe Schiedsrichter-Kollegen,

ich studiere an der Universität Bielefeld „Sportwissenschaft - Organisationsentwicklung und Management" (Master of Arts). Da ich nun kurz vor dem Abschluss des Studiums stehe, bin ich derzeitig damit beschäftigt, meine Masterarbeit zum Thema „Motivation von Schiedsrichtern im Amateurfußball" zu schreiben. Hierzu benötige ich Hilfe. Inhaltlich geht es in der Arbeit darum, zu analysieren, welche Motive Schiedsrichter haben, als Unparteiischer aktiv zu sein und welche Erfahrungen sie im Laufe ihrer Karriere gemacht haben. Um verlässliche Informationen zu erhalten, habe ich einen Fragebogen entwickelt. Ich würde mich sehr freuen, wenn ihr euch nun 20-30 Minuten Zeit nehmt und den folgenden Fragebogen ehrlich und gewissenhaft ausfüllt. Mit euren Antworten helft ihr nicht nur mir, sondern auch dem KSA, der auf diesem Weg wichtige Anregungen aus euren Reihen zur Verbesserung seiner Arbeit erhalten kann.

Besonders wichtig ist mir folgende Anmerkung: **Die Bögen werden absolut vertraulich und anonym behandelt!** Es wird also nicht ersichtlich sein, von welchem Schiedsrichter der jeweilige Fragebogen ausgefüllt wurde. Ihr könnt demnach absolut offen und ehrlich antworten!

Vielen Dank für die Hilfe!

Mit sportlichen Grüßen,

Michael Negri

1. Persönliche Angaben

1.1 Geschlecht

Bitte kreuzen Sie die zutreffende Antwort an!

Ich bin ☐ Weiblich ☐ Männlich

1.2 Alter

Bitte tragen Sie ihr <u>Alter</u> in die dafür vorgesehene Lücke ein!

Ich bin _____ Jahre alt.

1.3 Schulbildung

Bitte kreuzen Sie Ihren höchsten Schulabschluss an. Es ist nur eine Antwort möglich.

☐ Volksschule ☐ Hauptschulabschluss ☐ Mittlere Reife

☐ Fachabitur ☐ Abitur ☐ Kein Schulabschluss

1.4 Akademische Bildung

Sollten Sie nicht studieren/studiert haben, überspringen Sie bitte die Frage 1.4 und gehen direkt zum Punkt 1.5 über.

Sollten Sie studieren/studiert haben, kreuzen Sie bitte Ihren angestrebten/erlangten Abschluss an. Es ist nur eine Antwort möglich.

☐ Bachelor ☐ Master ☐ Staatsexamen/Staatsprüfung

☐ Diplom ☐ Magister ☐ Promotion

☐ Studium abgebrochen/Kein abgeschlossenes Studium

1.5 Beruflicher Status

Bitte kreuzen Sie hier Ihren beruflichen Status an. Es ist nur eine Antwort möglich. Sollte keine der genannten Antworten zutreffen, tragen Sie bitte Ihre Antwort unter „Sonstiges" ein.

☐ Schüler ☐ Zivildienstleistender ☐ Wehrdienstleistender

☐ Student ☐ Auszubildender ☐ Gewerblicher Angestellter

☐ Rentner ☐ Selbstständig ☐ Ungelernter Arbeiter

☐ Aushilfe ☐ Umschüler ☐ Arbeiter

☐ Kaufmännischer Angestellter ☐ Arbeitsuchend

☐ Sonstiges: _____

2. Schiedsrichtertätigkeit

2.1 Beginn der Schiedsrichtertätigkeit

Bitte tragen Sie in die dafür vorgesehene Lücke das Jahr ein, in dem Sie Ihre Schiedsrichtertätigkeit begonnen haben

Ich habe meine Schiedsrichtertätigkeit im Jahr _____ begonnen.

2.2 Karriere

Bitte kreuzen Sie die zutreffende Antwort an! Sollten Sie in bestimmten Bereichen nicht als Schiedsrichter tätig sein, kreuzen Sie bitte keine Antwort an. Pro Jugend-Altersklasse (F-, E-, D-, C-, B-, A-Junioren) ist nur die höchste Spielklasse anzukreuzen.

Die höchste Spielklasse, in der ich im <u>weiblichen Jugendbereich</u> als Schiedsrichter aktiv bin, ist die…

☐ B-Juniorinnen Kreisliga ☐ B-Juniorinnen Bezirksliga ☐ B-Juniorinnen Westfalenliga

Die höchste Spielklasse, in der ich im <u>männlichen Jugendbereich</u> als Schiedsrichter aktiv bin, ist die…

☐ C-, D-, E- ,F-Junioren Kreisliga ☐ C-Junioren Bezirksliga ☐ C-Junioren Landesliga

☐ C-Junioren Regionalliga ☐ B-Junioren Kreisliga ☐ B-Junioren Bezirksliga

☐ B-Junioren Landesliga ☐ B-Junioren Westfalenliga ☐ A-Junioren Kreisliga

☐ A-Junioren Bezirksliga ☐ A-Junioren Landesliga ☐ A-Junioren Westfalenliga

Die höchste Spielklasse, in der ich im <u>weiblichen Seniorenbereich</u> als Schiedsrichter aktiv bin, ist die…

☐ Kreisliga ☐ Bezirksliga ☐ Landesliga ☐ Verbandsliga ☐ Regionalliga

Die höchste Spielklasse, in der ich im <u>männlichen Seniorenbereich</u> als Schiedsrichter aktiv bin, ist die...

☐ Alte Herren (Ü 40) ☐ Alte Herren (Ü 32) ☐ Kreisliga C ☐ Kreisliga B

☐ Kreisliga A ☐ Bezirksliga ☐ Landesliga

☐ Westfalenliga (ehem. Verbandsliga) ☐ NRW-Liga (ehem. Oberliga) ☐ Regionalliga

2.3 Wie lange möchten Sie die Schiedsrichter-Tätigkeit noch fortsetzen?

Zutreffendes bitte ankreuzen. Es ist nur eine Antwort möglich.

Ich plane, noch...

☐ ...bis zu 6 Monaten als Schiedsrichter tätig zu sein

☐ ...zwischen 6 Monaten und 1 Jahr als Schiedsrichter tätig zu sein

☐ ...zwischen 1 Jahr und 5 Jahren als Schiedsrichter tätig zu sein

☐ ...zwischen 5 Jahren und 10 Jahren als Schiedsrichter tätig zu sein

☐ ...zwischen 10 Jahren und 15 Jahren als Schiedsrichter tätig zu sein

☐ ...zwischen 15 Jahren und 20 Jahren als Schiedsrichter tätig zu sein

☐ ...mehr als 20 Jahre als Schiedsrichter tätig zu sein

3. Motive/Beweggründe

Im folgenden Teil werden Aussagen zu bestimmten Gründen und Motiven gestellt. Bitte kreuzen Sie auf der Skala unter der jeweiligen Frage die Antwort an, die Sie für sich als passend erachten. Pro Aussage ist nur eine Antwort möglich.

Ich bin Schiedsrichter, weil...

...ich mich körperlich fit halten möchte

●————●————●————●————●

Trifft voll zu   Trifft eher zu   Weiss ich nicht   Trifft eher nicht zu   Trifft gar nicht zu

...ich Geld verdienen möchte

Trifft voll   Trifft   Weiss ich   Trifft eher   Trifft gar
zu   eher zu   nicht   nicht zu   nicht zu

...ich einen Ausgleich zu meinem Beruf suche

Trifft voll   Trifft   Weiss ich   Trifft eher   Trifft gar
zu   eher zu   nicht   nicht zu   nicht zu

...mich mein Verein überredet hat, Schiedsrichter zu sein und ich dem Verein helfen möchte, das Schiedsrichter-Soll zu erfüllen

Trifft voll   Trifft   Weiss ich   Trifft eher   Trifft gar
zu   eher zu   nicht   nicht zu   nicht zu

...Freunde und Bekannte, die Schiedsrichter sind, mir positiv davon berichtet haben

Trifft voll   Trifft   Weiss ich   Trifft eher   Trifft gar
zu   eher zu   nicht   nicht zu   nicht zu

...ich es mag, Verantwortung auf dem Spielfeld zu übernehmen

Trifft voll   Trifft   Weiss ich   Trifft eher   Trifft gar
zu   eher zu   nicht   nicht zu   nicht zu

...ich mich durch das Leiten der Spiele persönlich weiterentwickeln möchte

Trifft voll   Trifft   Weiss ich   Trifft eher   Trifft gar
zu   eher zu   nicht   nicht zu   nicht zu

...dies mein einziges Hobby ist

Trifft voll   Trifft   Weiss ich   Trifft eher   Trifft gar
zu   eher zu   nicht   nicht zu   nicht zu

...ich als aktiver Fußballer nicht gut genug war

| Trifft voll zu | Trifft eher zu | Weiss ich nicht | Trifft eher nicht zu | Trifft gar nicht zu |

... ich mit meinem Schiedsrichter-Ausweis kostenlos Bundesligaspiele im Stadion verfolgen kann

| Trifft voll zu | Trifft eher zu | Weiss ich nicht | Trifft eher nicht zu | Trifft gar nicht zu |

...ich mich vor meiner Tätigkeit als Schiedsrichter über deren Leistungen aufgeregt habe und es besser machen wollte als diese

| Trifft voll zu | Trifft eher zu | Weiss ich nicht | Trifft eher nicht zu | Trifft gar nicht zu |

...ich etwas Neues ausprobieren wollte

| Trifft voll zu | Trifft eher zu | Weiss ich nicht | Trifft eher nicht zu | Trifft gar nicht zu |

...ich hoffe, möglichst weit aufzusteigen

| Trifft voll zu | Trifft eher zu | Weiss ich nicht | Trifft eher nicht zu | Trifft gar nicht zu |

...ich mit meinem Schiedsrichter-Ausweis kostenlos Fußballspiele im Amateurbereich verfolgen kann

| Trifft voll zu | Trifft eher zu | Weiss ich nicht | Trifft eher nicht zu | Trifft gar nicht zu |

...ich gern unterwegs bin

| Trifft voll zu | Trifft eher zu | Weiss ich nicht | Trifft eher nicht zu | Trifft gar nicht zu |

…ich gern zeige, wer auf dem Platz der Chef ist

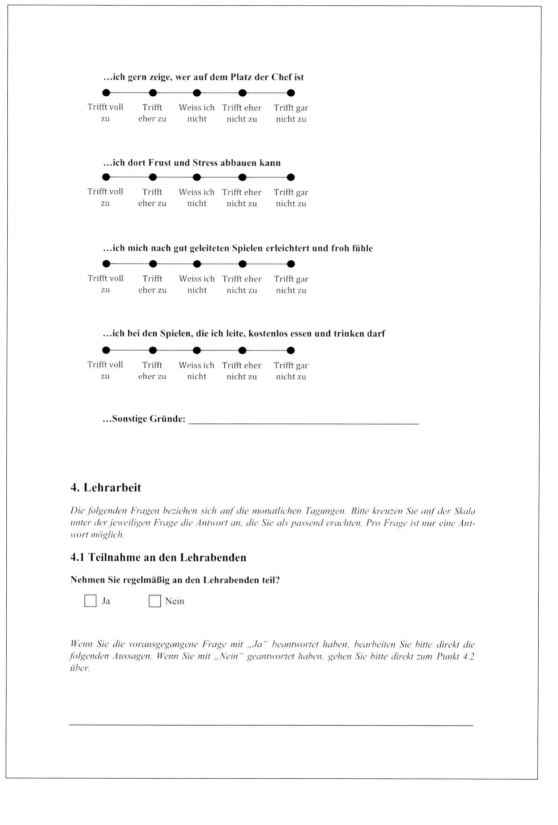

| Trifft voll zu | Trifft eher zu | Weiss ich nicht | Trifft eher nicht zu | Trifft gar nicht zu |

…ich dort Frust und Stress abbauen kann

| Trifft voll zu | Trifft eher zu | Weiss ich nicht | Trifft eher nicht zu | Trifft gar nicht zu |

…ich mich nach gut geleiteten Spielen erleichtert und froh fühle

| Trifft voll zu | Trifft eher zu | Weiss ich nicht | Trifft eher nicht zu | Trifft gar nicht zu |

…ich bei den Spielen, die ich leite, kostenlos essen und trinken darf

| Trifft voll zu | Trifft eher zu | Weiss ich nicht | Trifft eher nicht zu | Trifft gar nicht zu |

…Sonstige Gründe: _____

4. Lehrarbeit

Die folgenden Fragen beziehen sich auf die monatlichen Tagungen. Bitte kreuzen Sie auf der Skala unter der jeweiligen Frage die Antwort an, die Sie als passend erachten. Pro Frage ist nur eine Antwort möglich.

4.1 Teilnahme an den Lehrabenden

Nehmen Sie regelmäßig an den Lehrabenden teil?

☐ Ja   ☐ Nein

Wenn Sie die vorausgegangene Frage mit „Ja" beantwortet haben, bearbeiten Sie bitte direkt die folgenden Aussagen. Wenn Sie mit „Nein" geantwortet haben, gehen Sie bitte direkt zum Punkt 4.2 über.

An den monatlichen Tagungen nehme ich teil, weil...

...es Pflicht ist

Trifft voll zu | Trifft eher zu | Weiss ich nicht | Trifft eher nicht zu | Trifft gar nicht zu

...ich mich dort mit anderen Kollegen austauschen kann

Trifft voll zu | Trifft eher zu | Weiss ich nicht | Trifft eher nicht zu | Trifft gar nicht zu

...mich die Lehrinhalte interessieren

Trifft voll zu | Trifft eher zu | Weiss ich nicht | Trifft eher nicht zu | Trifft gar nicht zu

...ich dort etwas lernen kann

Trifft voll zu | Trifft eher zu | Weiss ich nicht | Trifft eher nicht zu | Trifft gar nicht zu

...ich sonst unattraktive Spiele leiten muss

Trifft voll zu | Trifft eher zu | Weiss ich nicht | Trifft eher nicht zu | Trifft gar nicht zu

...mir sonst langweilig wäre

Trifft voll zu | Trifft eher zu | Weiss ich nicht | Trifft eher nicht zu | Trifft gar nicht zu

...ich die Atmosphäre angenehm finde

Trifft voll zu | Trifft eher zu | Weiss ich nicht | Trifft eher nicht zu | Trifft gar nicht zu

...die Lehrinhalte gut und verständlich vermittelt werden

| Trifft voll zu | Trifft eher zu | Weiss ich nicht | Trifft eher nicht zu | Trifft gar nicht zu |

...die Lehrhinhalte interessant sind

| Trifft voll zu | Trifft eher zu | Weiss ich nicht | Trifft eher nicht zu | Trifft gar nicht zu |

...ich dort meine Regelkenntnisse unter Beweis stellen kann

| Trifft voll zu | Trifft eher zu | Weiss ich nicht | Trifft eher nicht zu | Trifft gar nicht zu |

...mein Verein ansonsten ein Ordnungsgeld zahlen muss

| Trifft voll zu | Trifft eher zu | Weiss ich nicht | Trifft eher nicht zu | Trifft gar nicht zu |

4.2 Abwesenheit bei Lehrabenden

Wenn ich an einem Lehrabend nicht teilnehme, liegt es normalerweise daran, dass ich...

...beruflich verhindert bin

| Immer | Oft | Manch-mal | Selten | Nie |

...keine Lust habe

| Immer | Oft | Manch-mal | Selten | Nie |

...ohnehin sowohl auf dem Platz als auch bei den Regelfragen sehr sicher bin

| Immer | Oft | Manch-mal | Selten | Nie |

...die Lehrarbeit als langweilig empfinde

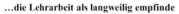

Immer   Oft   Manch-   Selten   Nie
                  mal

...die Kollegen nicht leiden kann

Immer   Oft   Manch-   Selten   Nie
                  mal

...keine Möglichkeit habe, dorthin zu fahren (kein Auto, Fahrrad, Mitfahrgelegenheit...)

Immer   Oft   Manch-   Selten   Nie
                  mal

...private Termine habe

Immer   Oft   Manch-   Selten   Nie
                  mal

... Zeit mit meiner Familie verbringen möchte

Immer   Oft   Manch-   Selten   Nie
                  mal

...den Termin vergesse

Immer   Oft   Manch-   Selten   Nie
                  mal

4.3 Regelmäßigkeit der Teilnahme

Die kommende Aussage bearbeiten bitte nur Schiedsrichter, die mindestens seit einem Jahr aktiv dabei sind. Alle anderen Schiedsrichter gehen bitte direkt zum Punkt 4.4 über.

Von den 10 Tagungen im Jahr nehme ich durchschnittlich an _____ Tagungen teil. *(Bitte hier die Anzahl der besuchten Tagungen pro Jahr in die Lücke eintragen)*

4.4 Meinung zu den Lehrabenden

Im folgenden Teil geht es um Ihre Meinung zu den monatlichen Lehrabenden. Bitte kreuzen Sie die passende Antwort an. Pro Aussage ist nur ein Kreuz möglich.

Die Lehrarbeit ist inhatlich interessant

| Trifft voll zu | Trifft eher zu | Weiss ich nicht | Trifft eher nicht zu | Trifft gar nicht zu |

Die Vortragsweise der Lehrwarte ist verständlich

| Trifft voll zu | Trifft eher zu | Weiss ich nicht | Trifft eher nicht zu | Trifft gar nicht zu |

Die Dauer der Lehrarbeit an einem Abend (jeweils circa 1 Stunde) ist passend

| Trifft voll zu | Trifft eher zu | Weiss ich nicht | Trifft eher nicht zu | Trifft gar nicht zu |

Der gesamte Lehrabend müsste kürzer sein

| Trifft voll zu | Trifft eher zu | Weiss ich nicht | Trifft eher nicht zu | Trifft gar nicht zu |

Die Dauer der Lehrarbeit müsste kürzer sein

| Trifft voll zu | Trifft eher zu | Weiss ich nicht | Trifft eher nicht zu | Trifft gar nicht zu |

Es müssten mehr Videoszenen zur Lehrarbeit gezeigt werden

| Trifft voll zu | Trifft eher zu | Weiss ich nicht | Trifft eher nicht zu | Trifft gar nicht zu |

Es müssten mehr Regeltests gemacht werden

| Trifft voll zu | Trifft eher zu | Weiss ich nicht | Trifft eher nicht zu | Trifft gar nicht zu |

Die Örtlichkeiten im Spexarder Bauernhaus sind passend für die Lehrabende

Trifft voll
zu
Trifft
eher zu
Weiss ich
nicht
Trifft eher
nicht zu
Trifft gar
nicht zu

Ich wünsche mir mehr Regelarbeit auf dem Spielfeld, damit ich mehr praktische Erfahrungen sammeln kann

Trifft voll
zu
Trifft
eher zu
Weiss ich
nicht
Trifft eher
nicht zu
Trifft gar
nicht zu

Der Termin am Montagabend passt mir zeitlich

Trifft voll
zu
Trifft
eher zu
Weiss ich
nicht
Trifft eher
nicht zu
Trifft gar
nicht zu

Die Stimmung an den Lehrabenden finde ich angenehm

Trifft voll
zu
Trifft
eher zu
Weiss ich
nicht
Trifft eher
nicht zu
Trifft gar
nicht zu

Ich wünsche mir, dass eine regelmäßige Teilnahme an den Lehrabenden zum Beispiel durch eine Ehrung am Saisonende belohnt wird

Trifft voll
zu
Trifft
eher zu
Weiss ich
nicht
Trifft eher
nicht zu
Trifft gar
nicht zu

Die Wahl zum „Schiedsrichter des Jahres" und „Jungschiedsrichter des Jahres" motiviert mich, regelmäßig an den Tagungen teilzunehmen

Trifft voll
zu
Trifft
eher zu
Weiss ich
nicht
Trifft eher
nicht zu
Trifft gar
nicht zu

5. Kreisliche Überprüfung

Die folgenden Fragen beziehen sich auf die jährlich stattfindende kreisliche Überprüfung.

An der kreislichen Überprüfung nehme ich im Normalfall teil

☐ Ja ☐ Nein

Wenn Sie die vorausgegangene Frage mit „Ja" beantwortet haben, gehen Sie bitte zu Punkt 5.1 über. Wenn Sie mit „Nein" geantwortet haben, gehen Sie bitte direkt zu Punkt 5.2 weiter.

Bitte kreuzen Sie auf der Skala unter der jeweiligen Frage die Antwort an, die Sie als passend erachten. Pro Frage ist nur eine Antwort möglich.

5.1 Teilnahme an der kreislichen Überprüfung

An der kreislichen Überprüfung nehme ich teil, weil...

...es Pflicht ist

| Trifft voll zu | Trifft eher zu | Weiss ich nicht | Trifft eher nicht zu | Trifft gar nicht zu |

...ich nicht in eine tiefere Spielklasse absteigen möchte

| Trifft voll zu | Trifft eher zu | Weiss ich nicht | Trifft eher nicht zu | Trifft gar nicht zu |

...ich in eine höhere Spielklasse aufsteigen möchte

| Trifft voll zu | Trifft eher zu | Weiss ich nicht | Trifft eher nicht zu | Trifft gar nicht zu |

...ich dort zeigen kann, was ich drauf habe

| Trifft voll zu | Trifft eher zu | Weiss ich nicht | Trifft eher nicht zu | Trifft gar nicht zu |

…ich sonst unattraktive Spiele leiten muss

| Trifft voll zu | Trifft eher zu | Weiss ich nicht | Trifft eher nicht zu | Trifft gar nicht zu |

…ich selbst herausfinden möchte, wie gut ich wirklich bin

| Trifft voll zu | Trifft eher zu | Weiss ich nicht | Trifft eher nicht zu | Trifft gar nicht zu |

…ich dort meine Regelkenntnisse unter Beweis stellen kann

| Trifft voll zu | Trifft eher zu | Weiss ich nicht | Trifft eher nicht zu | Trifft gar nicht zu |

…ich dort die anderen Kollegen wiedersehe

| Trifft voll zu | Trifft eher zu | Weiss ich nicht | Trifft eher nicht zu | Trifft gar nicht zu |

5.2 Fehlen bei der kreislichen Überprüfung

Im folgenden Teil geht es um die Gründe für das Fehlen bei der kreislichen Überprüfung. Bitte kreuzen Sie auf den Skalen unter der Aussage die treffende Antwort an, sofern Sie an der jährlichen Überprüfung nicht teilgenommen haben. Alle Schiedsrichter, die teilgenommen haben, gehen bitte direkt zum Punkt 6 über. Es ist jeweils nur eine Antwort möglich.

Bei der kreislichen Überprüfung habe ich gefehlt, weil…

…ich an keinem der Termine Zeit hatte

| Trifft voll zu | Trifft eher zu | Weiss ich nicht | Trifft eher nicht zu | Trifft gar nicht zu |

…ich Angst vor zu vielen Fehlern im Regeltest hatte

| Trifft voll zu | Trifft eher zu | Weiss ich nicht | Trifft eher nicht zu | Trifft gar nicht zu |

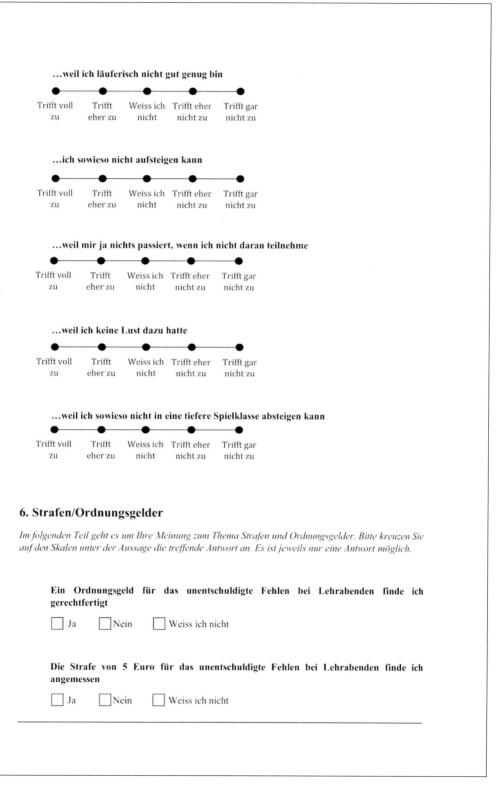

...weil ich läuferisch nicht gut genug bin

| Trifft voll zu | Trifft eher zu | Weiss ich nicht | Trifft eher nicht zu | Trifft gar nicht zu |

...ich sowieso nicht aufsteigen kann

| Trifft voll zu | Trifft eher zu | Weiss ich nicht | Trifft eher nicht zu | Trifft gar nicht zu |

...weil mir ja nichts passiert, wenn ich nicht daran teilnehme

| Trifft voll zu | Trifft eher zu | Weiss ich nicht | Trifft eher nicht zu | Trifft gar nicht zu |

...weil ich keine Lust dazu hatte

| Trifft voll zu | Trifft eher zu | Weiss ich nicht | Trifft eher nicht zu | Trifft gar nicht zu |

...weil ich sowieso nicht in eine tiefere Spielklasse absteigen kann

| Trifft voll zu | Trifft eher zu | Weiss ich nicht | Trifft eher nicht zu | Trifft gar nicht zu |

6. Strafen/Ordnungsgelder

Im folgenden Teil geht es um Ihre Meinung zum Thema Strafen und Ordnungsgelder. Bitte kreuzen Sie auf den Skalen unter der Aussage die treffende Antwort an. Es ist jeweils nur eine Antwort möglich.

Ein Ordnungsgeld für das unentschuldigte Fehlen bei Lehrabenden finde ich gerechtfertigt

☐ Ja ☐ Nein ☐ Weiss ich nicht

Die Strafe von 5 Euro für das unentschuldigte Fehlen bei Lehrabenden finde ich angemessen

☐ Ja ☐ Nein ☐ Weiss ich nicht

Die Strafe von 5 Euro für das unentschuldigte Fehlen bei Lehrabenden sollte höher sein, um wirksam zu sein

☐ Ja   ☐ Nein   ☐ Weiss ich nicht

Die Strafe von 5 Euro für das unentschuldigte Fehlen bei Lehrabenden schreckt mich ab. Ich komme also lieber zu den Lehrabenden

☐ Ja   ☐ Nein   ☐ Weiss ich nicht

Ein Ordnungsgeld für die Nicht-Teilnahme bei der kreislichen Überprüfung würde dazu führen, dass ich an der Prüfung teilnehme

☐ Ja   ☐ Nein   ☐ Weiss ich nicht

Ich finde es gerecht, dass ich in eine tiefere Spielklasse absteige, wenn ich an der kreislichen Überprüfung nicht teilnehme

☐ Ja   ☐ Nein   ☐ Weiss ich nicht

Die Strafen für das Fernbleiben an Lehrabenden und der kreislichen Überprüfung werden durch den Kreis-Schiedsrichterausschuss konsequent ausgesprochen

☐ Ja   ☐ Nein   ☐ Weiss ich nicht

Ein Ordnungsgeld für die zu kurzfristige Rückgabe von Spielen würde dazu führen, dass ich die Spiele eher zurückgebe

☐ Ja   ☐ Nein   ☐ Weiss ich nicht

Das Ordnungsgeld für das unentschuldigte Fernbleiben an Lehrabenden muss ich meinem Verein erstatten

☐ Ja   ☐ Nein

7. Spielleitungen

Im folgenden Teil geht es um Ihre Meinung zum Thema Spielleitungen. Bitte kreuzen Sie auf den Skalen unter der Aussage die treffende Antwort an. Es ist jeweils nur eine Antwort möglich.

7.1 Betreuung bei Spielleitungen

Ich glaube, dass andere Kollegen mir nützliche Hinweise zur Verbesserung meiner Spielleitungen geben könnten

| Trifft voll zu | Trifft eher zu | Weiss ich nicht | Trifft eher nicht zu | Trifft gar nicht zu |

Mir wäre es unangenehm, wenn mich Mitglieder des Kreis-Schiedsrichterausschusses bei meinen Spielleitungen beobachten und mir Tipps sowie Hinweise geben würden

| Trifft voll zu | Trifft eher zu | Weiss ich nicht | Trifft eher nicht zu | Trifft gar nicht zu |

Mich würde es motivieren, wenn mich Mitglieder des Kreis-Schiedsrichterausschusses bei meinen Spielleitungen beobachten und mir Tipps sowie Hinweise geben würden

| Trifft voll zu | Trifft eher zu | Weiss ich nicht | Trifft eher nicht zu | Trifft gar nicht zu |

Wenn ich von einem Mitglied des Kreis-Schiedsrichterausschusses beobachtet würde, würde ich das Spiel noch genauer nach den Regeln und Anweisungen leiten um keinen Ärger zu bekommen

| Trifft voll zu | Trifft eher zu | Weiss ich nicht | Trifft eher nicht zu | Trifft gar nicht zu |

7.2 Sonstige Vorkommnisse bei Spielleitungen

In diesem Kapitel werden Ihnen generelle Fragen zu Ihren Spielleitungen gestellt. Bitte kreuzen Sie zutreffende Antwort an. Es ist jeweils nur eine Antwort möglich.

Haben Sie bereits im Spielbericht eine im Spiel ausgesprochene rote Karte in eine gelb-rote umgewandelt?

☐ Ja ☐ Nein

Wenn Sie die vorausgegangene Frage mit „Ja" beantwortet haben, gehen Sie bitte zur nächsten Frage über. Wenn Sie mit „Nein" geantwortet haben, gehen Sie bitte direkt zur übernächsten Frage.

Wie oft haben Sie im Spielbericht eine im Spiel ausgesprochene rote Karte in eine gelb-rote umgewandelt?

Ich habe circa _____ mal eine rote Karte in eine gelb-rote Karte umgewandelt

Es wurde mir schon mal Geld angeboten, damit ich bewusst Entscheidungen zu Gunsten einer Mannschaft treffe

☐ Ja ☐ Nein

Wenn Sie die vorausgegangene Frage mit „Ja" beantwortet haben, beantworten Sie bitte auch die folgenden zwei Fragen. Wenn Sie mit „Nein" geantwortet haben, überspringen Sie bitte die folgenden zwei Fragen.

Bitte tragen Sie hier den Höchstbetrag in Euro ein, der Ihnen für die bewusste Bevorteilung einer Mannschaft geboten wurde.

Es wurden mir maximal _____ Euro für die Bevorteilung einer Mannschaft geboten.

Bitte tragen Sie hier die Anzahl der Spiele ein, bei denen Ihnen Geld für die bewusste Bevorteilung einer Mannschaft geboten wurde.

Es wurde mir bei circa _____ Spielen Geld für bewusste Bevorteilung einer Mannschaft geboten.

8. Sonstiges

Hier haben Sie die Möglichkeit, zu den bestimmten Sachverhalten Wünsche, Kritik und sonstige Anmerkungen zu äußern.

8.1 Lehrarbeit

_____

_____

8.2 Ansetzungen

_____

_____

8.3 Monatliche Tagung

_____

_____

8.4 Kreisliche Überprüfung

_____

_____

8.5 Kreis-Schiedsrichterausschuss

_____

_____

8.6 Spielleitungen

_____

_____

8.7 Erfahrungen mit Gewalt/Beleidigungen bei Spielleitungen

(Gab es das schon mal? Hat dies aus Ihrer Sicht in der Vergangenheit zugenommen? Was ist passiert? Was war Auslöser?)

_____

_____

Vielen Dank für die Teilnahme!

_____

STATA Commands

```
                  ___ ___ ___ ___ ___ tm
                 /_  /  __/ /  __/
               __/  /  /__/ /  /__/  10.0  Copyright 1984-2007
            Statistics/Data Analysis        StataCorp
                              4905 Lakeway Drive
                              College Station, Texas 77845 USA
                              800-STATA-PC      http://www.stata.com
                              979-696-4600      stata@stata.com
                              979-696-4601 (fax)
```

Unlimited-user Stata for Windows (network) perpetual license:
     Serial number: 44445530536
       Licensed to: Lalala
                 RRBK Bielefeld

Notes:
     1. (/m# option or -set memory-) 1.00 MB allocated to data
     2. New update available; type -update all-

. clear

.

. set more off

.

. set mem 200m
(204800k)

.

. capture log close

.

.

. *Log-Datei öffnen, um Ergebnisse zu sehen*

.

. log using "E:\Master-Studium\Masterthesis\Schiedsrichter-Arbeit\Fragebogen\STATA\Final Version - Referee Data.dta", replace
----
     log: E:\Master-Studium\Masterthesis\Schiedsrichter-Arbeit\Fragebogen\STATA\Final Version - Referee Data.dta
 log type: smcl
 opened on: 19 May 2010, 16:21:46

.

.

.

.

. *Import of the Data from the Questionnaire Study*

.

.

. use "E:\Master-Studium\Masterthesis\Schiedsrichter-Arbeit\Fragebogen\STATA\Referee Data.dta", clear

Creation of Dummy Variables: Age Groups and Classification of the Divisions

.
.
.
. gen Jugend = 0

.
.
.
. replace Jugend = 1 if hchstespielklassemnnlichersenior==0
(8 real changes made)

.
.
.
. gen Kreisebene = 0

.
.
. replace Kreisebene = 1 if hchstespielklassemnnlichersenior>=1 &
hchstespielklassemnnlichersenior<=5
(35 real changes made)

.
.
. gen UeberkreislicherSchiedsrichter = 0

.
.
. replace UeberkreislicherSchiedsrichter = 1 if hchstespielklassemnnlichersenior>=6 &
hchstespielklassemnnlichersenior<=9
(17 real changes made)

.
.
. gen Spielklasse = 0

.
.
. replace Spielklasse = 1 if Jugend==1
(8 real changes made)

.
.
. replace Spielklasse = 2 if Kreisebene==1
(35 real changes made)

.
.
. replace Spielklasse = 3 if UeberkreislicherSchiedsrichter==1
(17 real changes made)

```
. gen Sehrjung = 0

.

.

.

. replace Sehrjung = 1 if alter>=16 & alter<=25
(23 real changes made)

.

.

.

. gen Jung = 0

.

.

. replace Jung = 1 if alter>= 26 & alter<=35
(4 real changes made)

.

.

. gen Mittelalt = 0

.

.

. replace Mittelalt = 1 if alter>= 36 & alter<=45
(16 real changes made)

.

.

. gen Alt = 0

.

.

. replace Alt = 1 if alter>=46 & alter<=55
(10 real changes made)

.

.

. gen Sehralt = 0

.

.

. replace Sehralt = 1 if alter>=56 & alter<=69
(7 real changes made)

.

.

. gen Altersklasse = 0

.

.

. replace Altersklasse =1 if Sehrjung==1
(23 real changes made)
```

```
. replace Altersklasse =2 if Jung==1
(4 real changes made)

.

.

. replace Altersklasse =3 if Mittelalt==1
(16 real changes made)

.

.

. replace Altersklasse =4 if Alt==1
(10 real changes made)

.

.

. replace Altersklasse =5 if Sehralt==1
(7 real changes made)

.

. *Start of the Analysis*

.

.

.

.

. *The Referees' Motives*

.

.

. sum ichmichkrperlichfithaltenmchte ichgeldverdienenmchte icheinenausgleichzumeinemberuf
michmeinvereinberredethatschie freundeundbekanntedieschiedsri
ichesmagverantwortungaufdemspi ichmichdurchdasleitenderspiele diesmeineinzigeshobbyist
ichalsaktiverfuballernichtgutgen ichmitmeinemschiedsrichterausw
ichmichvormeinerttigkeitalssch ichetwasneuesausprobieren
> woll ichhoffemglichstweitaufzusteig mitausweiskostenlosamateursp ichgernunterwegsbin
ichgernzeigeweraufdemplatzderche ichdortfrustundstressabbauen ichmichnachgu
ichbeidenspielendieichleitekos

    Variable |    Obs    Mean   Std. Dev.    Min      Max
-------------+---------------------------------------------
ichmichkrp~e |     60  3.933333  1.162503      1       5
ichgeldver~e |     60  2.566667  1.357548      1       5
icheinenau~u |     60  2.916667  1.252681      1       5
michmeinve~s |     60  2.033333  1.248276      1       5
freundeund~h |     60     2.45  1.454683      1       5
-------------+---------------------------------------------
ichesmagve~l |     60  4.233333   .8309004     2       5
ichmichdur~e |     60      3.7  1.168804      1       5
diesmeinei~t |     60  2.166667  1.304057      1       5
ichalsakti~n |     60  2.383333  1.378917      1       5
ichmitmein~i |     60  2.383333  1.290009      1       5
-------------+---------------------------------------------
ichmichvor~e |     60      2.9  1.398546      1       5
ichetwasne~e |     60  3.366667  1.389631      1       5
ichhoffemg~n |     60     3.25  1.373169      1       5
mitausweis~e |     60     2.35  1.259876      1       5
ichgernunt~n |     60  3.066667  1.191306      1       5
-------------+---------------------------------------------
ichgernzei~e |     60  2.616667  1.249972      1       5
ichdortfru~n |     60  1.983333  1.185958      1       5
ichmichnac~e |     60  4.116667   .9404591     1       5
ichbeidens~e |     59  1.610169   .9100388     1       5
```

Regression: Motives and Age

.

.

. mvreg ichmichkrperlichfithaltenmchte ichgeldverdienenmchte icheinenausgleichzumeinemberuf
michmeinvereinberredethatschie freundeundbekanntediedschiedsri ichesmagverantwortungaufdemspi
ichmichdurchdasleitenderspiele diesmeineinzigeshobbyist ichalsaktiverfuballernichtgut ichmitmeinemschiedsrichterausw
ichmichvormeinerttigkeitalssch ichetwasneuesausprobierenwoll ichhoffemglichstweitaufzusteig
mitausweiskostenlosamateursp ichgernunterwegsbin ichgernzeigeweraufdemplatzderche ichdortfrustundstressabbauen
ichmichnachg ichbeidenspielendieichleitekos = Altersklasse

```
Equation      Obs Parms    RMSE    "R-sq"      F       P
---------------------------------------------------------------
ichmichkrp~e   59    2   1.03475   0.1402   9.295486   0.0035
ichgeldver~e   59    2   1.20239   0.2273  16.76429    0.0001
icheinenau~u   59    2   1.255589  0.0167   .9699329   0.3289
michmeinve~s   59    2   1.269704  0.0004   .0246622   0.8758
freundeund~h   59    2   1.464269  0.0016   .0905118   0.7646
ichesmagve~l   59    2    .8396481 0.0121   .698512    0.4068
ichmichdur~e   59    2   1.104084  0.0506  3.038025    0.0867
diesmeinei~t   59    2   1.278418  0.0388  2.298825    0.1350
ichalsakti~n   59    2   1.370276  0.0427  2.540535    0.1165
ichmitmein~i   59    2   1.285122  0.0397  2.359119    0.1301
ichmichvor~e   59    2   1.403855  0.0161   .930295    0.3389
ichetwasne~e   59    2   1.3051    0.1448  9.65086     0.0029
ichhoffemg~n   59    2   1.18723   0.2774  21.88272    0.0000
mitausweis~e   59    2   1.266263  0.0044   .2504823   0.6187
ichgernunt~n   59    2   1.158708  0.0732  4.504525    0.0382
ichgernzei~e   59    2   1.050781  0.2970  24.08156    0.0000
ichdortfru~n   59    2   1.175654  0.0008   .0464928   0.8301
ichmichnac~e   59    2    .8601047 0.0033   .1860273   0.6679
ichbeidens~e   59    2    .9036993 0.0309  1.816609    0.1831
```

```
---------------------------------------------------------------
        |  Coef.  Std. Err.   t   P>|t|   [95% Conf. Interval]
--------+------------------------------------------------------
ichmichkrp~e |
Altersklasse |  .2877079  .094366   3.05  0.003   .0987432  .4766727
       _cons |  3.236961  .2793412 11.59  0.000   2.67759   3.796332
--------+------------------------------------------------------
ichgeldver~e |
Altersklasse | -.448971   .1096543 -4.09  0.000  -.6685499 -.229392
       _cons |  3.706654  .3245973 11.42  0.000   3.056659  4.356648
--------+------------------------------------------------------
icheinenau~u |
Altersklasse |  .1127714  .1145059  0.98  0.329  -.1165228  .3420655
       _cons |  2.605864  .338959   7.69  0.000   1.92711   3.284618
--------+------------------------------------------------------
michmeinve~s |
Altersklasse | -.0181844  .1157932 -0.16  0.876  -.2500562  .2136874
       _cons |  2.081054  .3427695  6.07  0.000   1.39467   2.767438
--------+------------------------------------------------------
```

```
freundeund~h |
Altersklasse |  -.0401748  .1335369   -0.30  0.765   -.3075778   .2272282
       _cons |   2.527911  .3952942    6.40  0.000    1.736348   3.319474
-------------+----------------------------------------------------------------
ichesmagve~l |
Altersklasse |   .0639977  .0765734    0.84  0.407   -.0893378   .2173333
       _cons |   4.071328  .2266715   17.96  0.000    3.617426    4.52523
-------------+----------------------------------------------------------------
ichmichdur~e |
Altersklasse |  -.1755004  .1006891   -1.74  0.087   -.3771269   .0261261
       _cons |   4.200874  .2980587   14.09  0.000    3.604022   4.797726
-------------+----------------------------------------------------------------
diesmeinei~t |
Altersklasse |   .1767691  .1165879    1.52  0.135   -.0566941   .4102323
       _cons |   1.677192   .345122    4.86  0.000     .986097   2.368287
-------------+----------------------------------------------------------------
ichalsakti~n |
Altersklasse |   .1991824   .124965    1.59  0.116   -.0510557   .4494205
       _cons |   1.856357  .3699198    5.02  0.000    1.115606   2.597109
-------------+----------------------------------------------------------------
ichmitmein~i |
Altersklasse |  -.1800113  .1171992   -1.54  0.130   -.4146987   .0546762
       _cons |   2.856639  .3469318    8.23  0.000     2.16192   3.551358
-------------+----------------------------------------------------------------
ichmichvor~e |
Altersklasse |  -.1234846  .1280273   -0.96  0.339   -.3798549   .1328856
       _cons |   3.201579  .3789848    8.45  0.000    2.442675   3.960483
-------------+----------------------------------------------------------------
ichetwasne~e |
Altersklasse |  -.3697491  .1190211   -3.11  0.003   -.6080848  -.1314134
       _cons |   4.314773  .3523249   12.25  0.000    3.609255   5.020292
-------------+----------------------------------------------------------------
ichhoffemg~n |
Altersklasse |  -.5064844  .1082718   -4.68  0.000   -.7232949  -.2896738
       _cons |   4.567663  .3205049   14.25  0.000    3.925863   5.209463
-------------+----------------------------------------------------------------
mitausweis~e |
Altersklasse |   .0577953  .1154793    0.50  0.619    -.173448   .2890386
       _cons |   2.223005  .3418404    6.50  0.000    1.538482   2.907529
-------------+----------------------------------------------------------------
ichgernunt~n |
Altersklasse |   -.224274  .1056707   -2.12  0.038   -.4358759  -.0126721
       _cons |   3.666338  .3128051   11.72  0.000    3.039956   4.292719
-------------+----------------------------------------------------------------
ichgernzei~e |
Altersklasse |  -.4702566   .095828   -4.91  0.000   -.6621489  -.2783642
       _cons |   3.863547   .283669   13.62  0.000    3.295509   4.431584
-------------+----------------------------------------------------------------
ichdortfru~n |
Altersklasse |   .0231181   .107216    0.22  0.830   -.1915783   .2378146
       _cons |   1.889202  .3173796    5.95  0.000     1.25366   2.524744
-------------+----------------------------------------------------------------
ichmichnac~e |
Altersklasse |   .0338314  .0784389    0.43  0.668   -.1232399   .1909027
       _cons |   4.081759   .232194   17.58  0.000    3.616799    4.54672
-------------+----------------------------------------------------------------
ichbeidens~e |
Altersklasse |  -.1110798  .0824146   -1.35  0.183   -.2761122   .0539527
       _cons |   1.898224  .2439628    7.78  0.000    1.409697   2.386751
------------------------------------------------------------------------------
```

Regression: Motives and Division

.
.

. mvreg ichmichkrperlichfithaltenmchte ichgeldverdienenmchte icheinenausgleichzumeinemberuf michmeinvereinberredethatschi
> e freundeundbekanntedieschiedsri ichesmagverantwortungaufdemspi ichmichdurchdasleitenderspiele diesmeineinzigeshobbyist
> ichalsaktiverfuballernichtgut ichmitmeinemschiedsrichterausw ichmichvormeinerttigkeitalssch ichetwasneuesausprobierenw
> oll ichhoffemglichstweitaufzusteig mitausweiskostenlosamateursp ichgernunterwegsbin ichgernzeigeweraufdemplatzderche ic
> hdortfrustundstressabbauen ichmichnachg ichbeidenspielendieichleitekos = Spielklasse

Equation	Obs	Parms	RMSE	"R-sq"	F	P
ichmichkrp~e	59	2	1.115495	0.0008	.0452257	0.8323
ichgeldver~e	59	2	1.309021	0.0841	5.236228	0.0258
icheinenau~u	59	2	1.263154	0.0048	.2776992	0.6003
michmeinve~s	59	2	1.231091	0.0603	3.657922	0.0608
freundeund~h	59	2	1.463938	0.0020	.1162958	0.7343
ichesmagve~l	59	2	.8216059	0.0541	3.26041	0.0763
ichmichdur~e	59	2	1.130149	0.0052	.3005909	0.5857
diesmeinei~t	59	2	1.301147	0.0043	.2452797	0.6223
ichalsakti~n	59	2	1.353374	0.0661	4.036995	0.0493
ichmitmein~i	59	2	1.311082	0.0006	.0317687	0.8592
ichmichvor~e	59	2	1.414126	0.0016	.0917837	0.7630
ichetwasne~e	59	2	1.389872	0.0301	1.768327	0.1889
ichhoffemg~n	59	2	1.386638	0.0143	.8263137	0.3672
mitausweis~e	59	2	1.266293	0.0043	.2477096	0.6206
ichgernunt~n	59	2	1.203589	0.0001	.0031241	0.9556
ichgernzei~e	59	2	1.199242	0.0843	5.249055	0.0257
ichdortfru~n	59	2	1.176079	0.0001	.0052206	0.9427
ichmichnac~e	59	2	.8603052	0.0028	.1593711	0.6912
ichbeidens~e	59	2	.8980237	0.0430	2.562405	0.1150

	Coef.	Std. Err.	t	P>|t|	[95% Conf. Interval]	
ichmichkrp~e						
Spielklasse	.0495562	.2330265	0.21	0.832	-.4170713	.5161838
_cons	3.877219	.5184069	7.48	0.000	2.839127	4.915311
ichgeldver~e						
Spielklasse	-.6257396	.2734541	-2.29	0.026	-1.173322	-.0781573
_cons	3.878698	.6083448	6.38	0.000	2.660509	5.096888
icheinenau~u						
Spielklasse	-.1390533	.2638723	-0.53	0.600	-.6674484	.3893419
_cons	3.195266	.5870286	5.44	0.000	2.019762	4.370771
michmeinve~s						
Spielklasse	-.4918639	.2571744	-1.91	0.061	-1.006847	.0231189
_cons	3.08432	.5721279	5.39	0.000	1.938653	4.229986
freundeund~h						
Spielklasse	-.1042899	.3058161	-0.34	0.734	-.7166762	.5080963
_cons	2.64645	.6803397	3.89	0.000	1.284093	4.008806
ichesmagve~l						
Spielklasse	.3099112	.1716332	1.81	0.076	-.0337783	.6536007
_cons	3.575444	.381827	9.36	0.000	2.810848	4.340039

```
ichmichdur~e |
Spielklasse | -.1294379  .2360877  -0.55  0.586  -.6021954  .3433197
      _cons |  4.022189  .5252171   7.66  0.000   2.97046   5.073918
-------------+----------------------------------------------------------------
diesmeinei~t |
Spielklasse | -.1346154  .271809   -0.50  0.622  -.6789036  .4096728
      _cons |  2.423077  .6046852   4.01  0.000   1.212216  3.633938
-------------+----------------------------------------------------------------
ichalsakti~n |
Spielklasse |  .5680473  .2827193   2.01  0.049   .0019118  1.134183
      _cons |  1.159763  .6289568   1.84  0.070  -.099701   2.419228
-------------+----------------------------------------------------------------
ichmitmein~i |
Spielklasse | -.0488166  .2738845  -0.18  0.859  -.5972607  .4996276
      _cons |  2.494083  .6093023   4.09  0.000   1.273976  3.71419
-------------+----------------------------------------------------------------
ichmichvor~e |
Spielklasse | -.089497   .2954105  -0.30  0.763  -.6810463  .5020522
      _cons |  3.072485  .6571905   4.68  0.000   1.756484  4.388487
-------------+----------------------------------------------------------------
ichetwasne~e |
Spielklasse | -.3860947  .2903438  -1.33  0.189  -.9674981  .1953088
      _cons |  4.180473  .6459189   6.47  0.000   2.887043  5.473904
-------------+----------------------------------------------------------------
ichhoffemg~n |
Spielklasse | -.2633136  .2896682  -0.91  0.367  -.8433642  .316737
      _cons |  3.816568  .6444159   5.92  0.000   2.526147  5.106989
-------------+----------------------------------------------------------------
mitausweis~e |
Spielklasse |  .1316568  .2645282   0.50  0.621  -.3980517  .6613653
      _cons |  2.091716  .5884876   3.55  0.001   .9132898  3.270142
-------------+----------------------------------------------------------------
ichgernunt~n |
Spielklasse |  .0140533  .2514293   0.06  0.956  -.4894253  .5175318
      _cons |  3.054734  .5593471   5.46  0.000   1.93466   4.174807
-------------+----------------------------------------------------------------
ichgernzei~e |
Spielklasse | -.5739645  .2505212  -2.29  0.026  -1.075625  -.0723045
      _cons |  3.869822  .5573268   6.94  0.000   2.753795  4.98585
-------------+----------------------------------------------------------------
ichdortfru~n |
Spielklasse |  .0177515  .2456825   0.07  0.943  -.4742192  .5097222
      _cons |  1.911243  .5465622   3.50  0.001   .8167706  3.005715
-------------+----------------------------------------------------------------
ichmichnac~e |
Spielklasse |  .0717456  .1797174   0.40  0.691  -.2881324  .4316235
      _cons |  4.016272  .3998118  10.05  0.000   3.215663  4.816882
-------------+----------------------------------------------------------------
ichbeidens~e |
Spielklasse | -.3002959  .1875968  -1.60  0.115  -.675952   .0753603
      _cons |  2.251479  .4173408   5.39  0.000   1.415769  3.08719
------------------------------------------------------------------------------
```

Attitude towards the monthly Meeting

.
.

.
. sum dielehrarbeitistinhatlichinteres dievortragsweisederlehrwarteistv diedauerderlehrarbeitaneinemaben dergesamtelehrab
> endmsstekrzersei diedauerderlehrarbeitmsstekrzers esmsstenmehrvideoszenenzurlehrar esmsstenmehrregeltestsgemachtwer die
> rtlichkeitenimspexarderbauern ichwnschemirmehrregelarbeitaufde derterminammontagabendpasstmirze diestimmungandenlehrabe
> ndenfinde ichwnschemirdasseineregelmigetei diewahlzumschiedsrichterdesjahre

Variable	Obs	Mean	Std. Dev.	Min	Max
dielehrarb~s	60	3.8	.8791367	1	5
dievortrag~v	60	4.083333	.8086747	2	5
diedauerde~n	60	3.866667	1.032796	1	5
dergesamte~i	60	2.816667	1.268813	1	5
diedauerde~s	60	2.5	1.049617	1	5
esmsstenm~ar	60	3.833333	1.076193	1	5
esmsstenm~er	60	3	1.089239	1	5
diertlichk~n	60	4.283333	.8653728	1	5
ichwnschem~e	60	3.366667	1.149306	1	5
dertermina~e	60	3.9	.9513594	1	5
diestimmun~e	60	3.916667	.6712414	2	5
ichwnschem~i	60	3.2	1.312263	1	5
diewahlzum~e	60	2.916667	1.369048	1	5

.
.
.
.

. *Regression: Attitude towards the monthly Meeting and Age*

.
.

. mvreg dielehrarbeitistinhatlichinteres dievortragsweisederlehrwarteistv diedauerderlehrarbeitaneinemaben dergesamtelehr
> abendmsstekrzersei diedauerderlehrarbeitmsstekrzers esmsstenmehrvideoszenenzurlehrar esmsstenmehrregeltestsgemachtwer d
> iertlichkeitenimspexarderbauern ichwnschemirmehrregelarbeitaufde derterminammontagabendpasstmirze diestimmungandenlehra
> bendenfinde ichwnschemirdasseineregelmigetei diewahlzumschiedsrichterdesjahre = Altersklasse

Equation	Obs	Parms	RMSE	"R-sq"	F	P
dielehrarb~s	60	2	.8482016	0.0849	5.382106	0.0239
dievortrag~v	60	2	.8153268	0.0007	.0411962	0.8399
diedauerde~n	60	2	1.003622	0.0717	4.479851	0.0386
dergesamte~i	60	2	1.164525	0.1719	12.04064	0.0010
diedauerde~s	60	2	1.001273	0.1054	6.834844	0.0114
esmsstenm~ar	60	2	1.032176	0.0957	6.139387	0.0162
esmsstenm~er	60	2	1.07526	0.0420	2.544004	0.1161
diertlichk~n	60	2	.8695329	0.0075	.4368071	0.5113
ichwnschem~e	60	2	1.142623	0.0283	1.692166	0.1985
dertermina~e	60	2	.9515753	0.0165	.9732353	0.3280
diestimmun~e	60	2	.6706068	0.0188	1.111719	0.2961
ichwnschem~i	60	2	1.304635	0.0283	1.691901	0.1985
diewahlzum~e	60	2	1.374443	0.0092	.5378131	0.4663

```
--------------------------------------------------------------
         | Coef.  Std. Err.    t    P>|t|   [95% Conf. Interval]
---------+----------------------------------------------------
dielehrarb~s |
Altersklasse | .1776209  .0765628   2.32  0.024   .0243638   .330878
       _cons | 3.344106  .2249609  14.87  0.000   2.893798  3.794415
---------+----------------------------------------------------
dievortrag~v |
Altersklasse | -.0149375 .0735954  -0.20  0.840  -.1622547  .1323796
       _cons | 4.121673  .2162418  19.06  0.000   3.688818  4.554528
---------+----------------------------------------------------
diedauerde~n |
Altersklasse | .1917436  .0905918   2.12  0.039   .0104043  .3730829
       _cons | 3.374525  .2661818  12.68  0.000   2.841704  3.907345
---------+----------------------------------------------------
dergesamte~i |
Altersklasse | -.3647474 .1051156  -3.47  0.001  -.5751593 -.1543356
       _cons | 3.752852  .3088564  12.15  0.000   3.134608  4.371095
---------+----------------------------------------------------
diedauerde~s |
Altersklasse | -.2362846 .0903798  -2.61  0.011  -.4171994 -.0553699
       _cons | 3.106464  .2655586  11.70  0.000   2.574891  3.638037
---------+----------------------------------------------------
esmsstenm~ar |
Altersklasse | -.2308528 .0931693  -2.48  0.016  -.4173513 -.0443543
       _cons | 4.425856  .2737549  16.17  0.000   3.877876  4.973835
---------+----------------------------------------------------
esmsstenm~er |
Altersklasse | .1548072  .0970582   1.59  0.116  -.0394759  .3490902
       _cons | 2.602662  .2851816   9.13  0.000   2.031809  3.173515
---------+----------------------------------------------------
diertlichk~n |
Altersklasse | .051874   .0784883   0.66  0.511  -.1052374  .2089853
       _cons | 4.15019   .2306184  18.00  0.000   3.688557  4.611823
---------+----------------------------------------------------
ichwnschem~e |
Altersklasse | -.1341662 .1031387  -1.30  0.198  -.3406208  .0722883
       _cons | 3.711027  .3030477  12.25  0.000   3.104411  4.317642
---------+----------------------------------------------------
dertermina~e |
Altersklasse | .0847366  .0858938   0.99  0.328  -.0871986  .2566717
       _cons | 3.68251   .2523778  14.59  0.000   3.17732   4.187699
---------+----------------------------------------------------
diestimmun~e |
Altersklasse | .063824   .0605322   1.05  0.296  -.0573444  .1849924
       _cons | 3.752852  .177859   21.10  0.000   3.396828  4.108875
---------+----------------------------------------------------
ichwnschem~i |
Altersklasse | -.1531776 .1177627  -1.30  0.198  -.3889053  .0825501
       _cons | 3.593156  .3460168  10.38  0.000   2.900528  4.285784
---------+----------------------------------------------------
diewahlzum~e |
Altersklasse | -.0909832 .1240639  -0.73  0.466  -.339324   .1573577
       _cons | 3.15019   .3645311   8.64  0.000   2.420502  3.879878
--------------------------------------------------------------
```

Regression: Attitude towards the monthly Meeting and Division

.

.

. mvreg dielehrarbeitistinhatlichinteres dievortragsweisederlehrwarteistv diedauerderlehrarbeitaneinemaben dergesamtelehr
> abendmsstekrzersei diedauerderlehrarbeitmsstekrzers esmsstenmehrvideoszenenzurlehrar esmsstenmehrregeltestsgemachtwer d
> iertlichkeitenimspexarderbauern ichwnschemirmehrregelarbeitaufde derterminammontagabendpasstmirze diestimmungandenlehra
> bendenfinde ichwnschemirdasseineregelmigetei diewahlzumschiedsrichterdesjahre = Spielklasse

```
Equation        Obs  Parms   RMSE      "R-sq"      F         P
-------------------------------------------------------------------
dielehrarb~s     60    2    .8864199   0.0006    .0344405   0.8534
dievortrag~v     60    2    .810882    0.0116    .6792353   0.4132
diedauerde~n     60    2    1.038071   0.0069    .4018041   0.5287
dergesamte~i     60    2    1.279584   0.0002    .0109108   0.9172
diedauerde~s     60    2    1.0544     0.0080    .4659016   0.4976
esmsstenm~ar     60    2    1.085347   0.0002    .0089737   0.9249
esmsstenm~er     60    2    1.021208   0.1359   9.122684    0.0038
diertlichk~n     60    2    .8644913   0.0190   1.120386    0.2942
ichwnschem~e     60    2    1.155742   0.0059    .3447268   0.5594
dertermina~e     60    2    .9563256   0.0067    .3888242   0.5354
diestimmun~e     60    2    .6693889   0.0224   1.327011    0.2541
ichwnschem~i     60    2    1.323131   0.0006    .0347797   0.8527
diewahlzum~e     60    2    1.366854   0.0201   1.189599    0.2799
```

```
            |    Coef.    Std. Err.    t     P>|t|    [95% Conf. Interval]
------------+------------------------------------------------------------
dielehrarb~s |
Spielklasse |  .0338266   .1822737   0.19   0.853   -.3310338    .398687
      _cons |  3.727273   .4082551   9.13   0.000    2.910061   4.544484
------------+------------------------------------------------------------
dievortrag~v |
Spielklasse |  .1374207   .1667409   0.82   0.413   -.1963474   .4711888
      _cons |  3.787879   .3734648  10.14   0.000    3.040308    4.53545
------------+------------------------------------------------------------
diedauerde~n |
Spielklasse |  .1353066   .2134576   0.63   0.529   -.2919753   .5625884
      _cons |  3.575758   .4781006   7.48   0.000    2.618735    4.53278
------------+------------------------------------------------------------
dergesamte~i |
Spielklasse |  .0274841   .2631197   0.10   0.917   -.4992071   .5541754
      _cons |  2.757576   .5893332   4.68   0.000    1.577897   3.937254
------------+------------------------------------------------------------
diedauerde~s |
Spielklasse | -.1479915   .2168152  -0.68   0.498   -.5819944   .2860113
      _cons |  2.818182   .4856209   5.80   0.000    1.846106   3.790258
------------+------------------------------------------------------------
esmsstenm~ar |
Spielklasse | -.0211416   .2231789  -0.09   0.925   -.4678828   .4255995
      _cons |  3.878788   .4998742   7.76   0.000    2.878181   4.879395
------------+------------------------------------------------------------
esmsstenm~er |
Spielklasse |  .6342495   .2099901   3.02   0.004    .2139086   1.05459
      _cons |  1.636364   .470334    3.48   0.001    .6948878   2.57784
------------+------------------------------------------------------------
diertlichk~n |
Spielklasse |  .1881607   .1777645   1.06   0.294   -.1676736   .543995
      _cons |  3.878788   .3981554   9.74   0.000    3.081793   4.675783
------------+------------------------------------------------------------
ichwnschem~e |
Spielklasse | -.1395349   .2376541  -0.59   0.559   -.6152512   .3361814
      _cons |  3.666667   .5322956   6.89   0.000    2.601161   4.732172
------------+------------------------------------------------------------
dertermina~e |
Spielklasse |  .1226216   .1966483   0.62   0.535   -.2710128   .5162559
      _cons |  3.636364   .4404512   8.26   0.000    2.754705   4.518023
------------+------------------------------------------------------------
diestimmun~e |
Spielklasse |  .1585624   .1376458   1.15   0.254   -.1169656   .4340903
      _cons |  3.575758   .3082979  11.60   0.000    2.958632   4.192883
------------+------------------------------------------------------------
ichwnschem~i |
Spielklasse |  .05074     .272074    0.19   0.853   -.4938754   .5953553
      _cons |  3.090909   .6093892   5.07   0.000    1.871084   4.310734
------------+------------------------------------------------------------
diewahlzum~e |
Spielklasse | -.3065539   .2810649  -1.09   0.280   -.8691664   .2560586
      _cons |  3.575758   .6295268   5.68   0.000    2.315623   4.835892
------------+------------------------------------------------------------
```

"Reasons for the Participation in the monthly Meeting"

.

.

. sum espflichtist ichmichdortmitanderenkollegenaus michdielehrinhalteinteressieren ichdortetwaslernenkann ichsonstunattr
> aktivespieleleiten mirsonstlangweiligwre ichdieatmosphreangenehmfinde dielehrinhaltegutundverstndlichv dielehrhinhaltei
> nteressantsind ichdortmeineregelkenntnisseeunter meinvereinamsonsteneinordnungsge

Variable	Obs	Mean	Std. Dev.	Min	Max
espflichtist	54	4.092593	1.068741	1	5
ichmichdor~s	54	3.814815	1.304189	1	5
michdieleh~n	54	4.12963	.9914026	1	5
ichdortetw~n	54	4.314815	.8201259	2	5
ichsonstun~n	54	2.277778	1.294643	1	5
mirsonstla~e	54	1.592593	1.000349	1	5
ichdieatmo~e	54	3.462963	1.076559	1	5
dielehrinh~v	54	3.740741	1.031306	1	5
dielehrhin~d	54	3.814815	.9126795	1	5
ichdortmei~r	54	3.685185	1.060866	1	5
meinverein~e	54	2.388889	1.534714	1	5

"Regression: Reasons for the Participation in the monthly Meeting and Age"

.

.

. mvreg espflichtist ichmichdortmitanderenkollegenaus michdielehrinhalteinteressieren ichdortetwaslernenkann ichsonstunat
> traktivespieleleiten mirsonstlangweiligwre ichdieatmosphreangenehmfinde dielehrinhaltegutundverstndlichv dielehrhinhalt
> einteressantsind ichdortmeineregelkenntnisseeunter meinvereinamsonsteneinordnungsge = Altersklasse

Equation	Obs	Parms	RMSE	"R-sq"	F	P
espflichtist	54	2	1.077959	0.0019	.0975118	0.7561
ichmichdor~s	54	2	1.316082	0.0009	.0463904	0.8303
michdieleh~n	54	2	.9059308	0.1807	11.47255	0.0014
ichdortetw~n	54	2	.7257689	0.2316	15.67686	0.0002
ichsonstun~n	54	2	1.275363	0.0479	2.614522	0.1119
mirsonstla~e	54	2	1.002058	0.0155	.8194238	0.3695
ichdieatmo~e	54	2	1.069922	0.0309	1.659623	0.2034
dielehrinh~v	54	2	1.041173	0.0000	.0001853	0.9892
dielehrhin~d	54	2	.8965129	0.0533	2.928714	0.0930
ichdortmei~r	54	2	.9997164	0.1287	7.681996	0.0077
meinverein~e	54	2	1.54396	0.0070	.3670708	0.5472

	Coef.	Std. Err.	t	P>|t|	[95% Conf. Interval]	
espflichtist						
Altersklasse	-.0322034	.1031271	-0.31	0.756	-.2391431	.1747364
_cons	4.179661	.3150586	13.27	0.000	3.54745	4.811872
ichmichdor~s						
Altersklasse	-.0271186	.1259082	-0.22	0.830	-.2797719	.2255346
_cons	3.888136	.3846559	10.11	0.000	3.116267	4.660004
michdieleh~n						
Altersklasse	.2935593	.0866694	3.39	0.001	.1196444	.4674742
_cons	3.335932	.2647794	12.60	0.000	2.804613	3.867251
ichdortetw~n						
Altersklasse	.2749153	.0694335	3.96	0.000	.1355867	.4142438
_cons	3.571525	.2121229	16.84	0.000	3.14587	3.997181
ichsonstun~n						
Altersklasse	-.1972881	.1220126	-1.62	0.112	-.4421244	.0475481
_cons	2.811186	.3727547	7.54	0.000	2.063199	3.559174
mirsonstla~e						
Altersklasse	.0867797	.0958658	0.91	0.370	-.1055891	.2791484
_cons	1.357966	.2928748	4.64	0.000	.7702697	1.945662
ichdieatmo~e						
Altersklasse	.1318644	.1023583	1.29	0.203	-.0735325	.3372613
_cons	3.106441	.3127097	9.93	0.000	2.478943	3.733939
dielehrinh~v						
Altersklasse	-.0013559	.0996079	-0.01	0.989	-.2012338	.198522
_cons	3.744407	.3043072	12.30	0.000	3.13377	4.355044
dielehrhin~d						
Altersklasse	.1467797	.0857684	1.71	0.093	-.0253273	.3188866
_cons	3.417966	.2620268	13.04	0.000	2.892171	3.943761
ichdortmei~r						
Altersklasse	.2650847	.0956418	2.77	0.008	.0731655	.457004
_cons	2.968475	.2921905	10.16	0.000	2.382151	3.554798
meinverein~e						
Altersklasse	-.0894915	.147709	-0.61	0.547	-.3858914	.2069083
_cons	2.630847	.4512585	5.83	0.000	1.725331	3.536364

Regression: Reasons for the Participation in the monthly Meeting and Division

.
.

. mvreg espflichtist ichmichdortmitanderenkollegenaus michdielehrinhalteinteressieren ichdortetwaslernenkann ichsonstunat
> traktivespieleleiten mirsonstlangweiligwre ichdieatmosphreangenehmfinde dielehrinhaltegutundverstndlichv dielehrhinhalt
> einteressantsind ichdortmeineregelkenntnisseunter meinvereinansonsteneinordnungsge = Spielklasse

```
Equation      Obs Parms    RMSE     "R-sq"       F       P
-----------------------------------------------------------------
espflichtist   54   2   1.07894   0.0001   .002774  0.9582
ichmichdor~s   54   2   1.315899  0.0012   .060894  0.8061
michdieleh~n   54   2   .9894565  0.0227   1.208693 0.2767
ichdortetw~n   54   2   .8267488  0.0030   .1542669 0.6961
ichsonstun~n   54   2   1.288465  0.0282   1.509468 0.2248
mirsonstla~e   54   2   1.007585  0.0046   .241544  0.6252
ichdieatmo~e   54   2   1.074873  0.0219   1.166428 0.2851
dielehrinh~v   54   2   1.041173  0.0000   .0002432 0.9876
dielehrhin~d   54   2   .9203125  0.0024   .1244942 0.7256
ichdortmei~r   54   2   1.070023  0.0019   .0967568 0.7570
meinverein~e   54   2   1.541592  0.0101   .5281037 0.4707
```

```
            |   Coef.  Std. Err.    t   P>|t|    [95% Conf. Interval]
------------+----------------------------------------------------------
espflichtist |
Spielklasse |  .0124555  .2364891   0.05  0.958  -.4620945  .4870055
      _cons |  4.065836  .5288056   7.69  0.000   3.00471   5.126962
------------+----------------------------------------------------------
ichmichdor~s |
Spielklasse |  .0711744  .2884273   0.25  0.806  -.5075973  .649946
      _cons |  3.661922  .644943    5.68  0.000   2.367749  4.956094
------------+----------------------------------------------------------
michdieleh~n |
Spielklasse |  .2384342  .2168755   1.10  0.277  -.1967583  .6736266
      _cons |  3.617438  .4849483   7.46  0.000   2.644318  4.590558
------------+----------------------------------------------------------
ichdortetw~n |
Spielklasse |  .0711744  .1812121   0.39  0.696  -.2924544  .4348031
      _cons |  4.161922  .4052027  10.27  0.000   3.348823  4.97502
------------+----------------------------------------------------------
ichsonstun~n |
Spielklasse | -.3469751  .2824141  -1.23  0.225  -.9136805  .2197303
      _cons |  3.023132  .6314971   4.79  0.000   1.75594   4.290323
------------+----------------------------------------------------------
mirsonstla~e |
Spielklasse |  .1085409  .220849    0.49  0.625  -.3346249  .5517068
      _cons |  1.359431  .4938333   2.75  0.008   .3684816  2.35038
------------+----------------------------------------------------------
ichdieatmo~e |
Spielklasse |  .2544484  .2355976   1.08  0.285  -.2183127  .7272095
      _cons |  2.91637   .5268122   5.54  0.000   1.859244  3.973496
------------+----------------------------------------------------------
dielehrinh~v |
Spielklasse |  .0035587  .228211    0.02  0.988  -.4543801  .4614975
      _cons |  3.733096  .5102952   7.32  0.000   2.709114  4.757078
------------+----------------------------------------------------------
dielehrhin~d |
Spielklasse |  .0711744  .20172     0.35  0.726  -.3336065  .4759552
      _cons |  3.661922  .4510597   8.12  0.000   2.756804  4.567039
------------+----------------------------------------------------------
ichdortmei~r |
Spielklasse |  .0729537  .2345346   0.31  0.757  -.3976743  .5435818
      _cons |  3.52847   .5244352   6.73  0.000   2.476113  4.580826
------------+----------------------------------------------------------
meinverein~e |
Spielklasse | -.2455516  .3378961  -0.73  0.471  -.9235897  .4324865
      _cons |  2.91637   .7555586   3.86  0.000   1.400231  4.432509
------------+----------------------------------------------------------
```

"Reasons for not participating in the monthly Meeting"

.

.

. sum beruflichverhindertbin keinelusthabe ohnehinsowohlaufdemplatzalsauchb dielehrarbeitalslangweiligempfin diekollegenn
> ichtleidenkann keinemglichkeithabedorthinzufahr privateterminehabe zeitmitmeinerfamilieverbringenmc denterminvergesse

Variable	Obs	Mean	Std. Dev.	Min	Max
beruflichv~n	56	2.714286	1.20173	1	5
keinelusth~e	56	1.910714	.9200155	1	5
ohnehinsow~b	56	2.714286	1.357997	1	5
dielehrarb~n	56	2.107143	1.12296	1	5
diekollege~n	56	1.285714	.5629237	1	4
keinemglic~r	56	1.428571	.7829349	1	4
privateter~e	56	2.535714	.8520411	1	5
zeitmitmei~c	56	2.285714	.9669876	1	5
denterminv~e	56	1.714286	.8678979	1	4

.

.

.

. "Regression: Reasons for not participating in the monthly Meeting and Age"

.

. mvreg beruflichverhindertbin keinelusthabe ohnehinsowohlaufdemplatzalsauchb dielehrarbeitalslangweiligempfin diekollege
> nnichtleidenkann keinemglichkeithabedorthinzufahr privateterminehabe zeitmitmeinerfamilieverbringenmc denterminvergesse
> = Altersklasse

Equation	Obs	Parms	RMSE	"R-sq"	F	P
beruflichv~n	56	2	1.212652	0.0003	.0137725	0.9070
keinelusth~e	56	2	.9006225	0.0591	3.394123	0.0709
ohnehinsow~b	56	2	1.363074	0.0108	.5910574	0.4454
dielehrarb~n	56	2	1.105591	0.0483	2.741717	0.1036
diekollege~n	56	2	.5677819	0.0012	.0628233	0.8030
keinemglic~r	56	2	.7471731	0.1058	6.390894	0.0144
privateter~e	56	2	.807102	0.1190	7.295271	0.0092
zeitmitmei~c	56	2	.9491052	0.0542	3.092069	0.0843
denterminv~e	56	2	.7662691	0.2347	16.55655	0.0002

	Coef.	Std. Err.	t	P>|t|	[95% Conf. Interval]	
beruflichv~n						
Altersklasse	.0128881	.1098205	0.12	0.907	-.2072887	.2330649
_cons	2.681605	.3221906	8.32	0.000	2.035652	3.327558
keinelusth~e						
Altersklasse	-.1502636	.0815624	-1.84	0.071	-.3137864	.0132592
_cons	2.29174	.2392872	9.58	0.000	1.811998	2.771482
ohnehinsow~b						
Altersklasse	.0949033	.1234431	0.77	0.445	-.1525851	.3423918
_cons	2.473638	.3621564	6.83	0.000	1.747558	3.199718
dielehrarb~n						
Altersklasse	-.1657879	.1001248	-1.66	0.104	-.366526	.0349502
_cons	2.527534	.2937454	8.60	0.000	1.93861	3.116458
diekollege~n						
Altersklasse	-.0128881	.0514196	-0.25	0.803	-.1159782	.090202
_cons	1.318395	.1508545	8.74	0.000	1.01595	1.62084
keinemglic~r						
Altersklasse	-.1710603	.0676657	-2.53	0.014	-.3067219	-.0353988
_cons	1.862332	.1985171	9.38	0.000	1.464329	2.260334
privateter~e						
Altersklasse	-.1974224	.073093	-2.70	0.009	-.343965	-.0508798
_cons	3.036321	.2144397	14.16	0.000	2.606395	3.466247
zeitmitmei~c						
Altersklasse	.1511424	.0859531	1.76	0.084	-.0211833	.323468
_cons	1.90246	.2521687	7.54	0.000	1.396893	2.408028
denterminv~e						
Altersklasse	-.2823667	.0693951	-4.07	0.000	-.4214954	-.143238
_cons	2.430287	.2035908	11.94	0.000	2.022112	2.838462

Regression: Reasons for not participating in the monthly Meeting and Division

.
.

. mvreg beruflichverhindertbin keinelusthabe ohnehinsowohlaufdemplatzalsauchb dielehrarbeitalslangweiligempfin diekollege
> nnichtleidenkann keinemglichkeithabedorthinzufahr privateterminehabe zeitmitmeinerfamilieverbringenmc denterminvergesse
> = Spielklasse

```
Equation      Obs  Parms    RMSE    "R-sq"      F       P
-------------------------------------------------------------------
beruflichv~n    56   2   1.210661  0.0035  .1915344  0.6634
keinelusth~e    56   2    .921009  0.0161  .8814042  0.3520
ohnehinsow~b    56   2   1.368821  0.0025  .1336448  0.7161
dielehrarb~n    56   2   1.132938  0.0007  .0354822  0.8513
diekollege~n    56   2   .5664008  0.0060  .3268021  0.5699
keinemglic~r    56   2   .7501065  0.0988  5.919496  0.0183
privateter~e    56   2   .8598796  0.0000   .001831  0.9660
zeitmitmei~c    56   2   .9591083  0.0341  1.907378  0.1729
denterminv~e    56   2   .8747881  0.0025   .137002  0.7127
```

```
             |   Coef.   Std. Err.     t    P>|t|    [95% Conf. Interval]
-------------+---------------------------------------------------------------
beruflichv~n |
 Spielklasse |  .1091736  .2494562   0.44  0.663  -.3909559   .6093031
       _cons |  2.478393  .5627593   4.40  0.000   1.350128   3.606657
-------------+---------------------------------------------------------------
keinelusth~e |
 Spielklasse | -.1781653  .1897735  -0.94  0.352  -.5586382   .2023076
       _cons |  2.295679  .4281184   5.36  0.000   1.437353   3.154004
-------------+---------------------------------------------------------------
ohnehinsow~b |
 Spielklasse | -.1031084  .2820448  -0.37  0.716  -.6685742   .4623574
       _cons |  2.937074  .6362775   4.62  0.000   1.661414   4.212733
-------------+---------------------------------------------------------------
dielehrarb~n |
 Spielklasse |  .0439727  .2334413   0.19  0.851  -.4240489   .5119943
       _cons |   2.01213  .5266306   3.82  0.000   .9562996   3.067961
-------------+---------------------------------------------------------------
diekollege~n |
 Spielklasse | -.0667172  .1167066  -0.57  0.570  -.3006999   .1672654
       _cons |  1.429871  .2632836   5.43  0.000   .9020192   1.957723
-------------+---------------------------------------------------------------
keinemglic~r |
 Spielklasse | -.3760425  .1545591  -2.43  0.018  -.6859148  -.0661702
       _cons |  2.241092  .3486767   6.43  0.000   1.542037   2.940146
-------------+---------------------------------------------------------------
privateter~e |
 Spielklasse |  .0075815  .1771778   0.04  0.966  -.3476386   .3628016
       _cons |  2.519333  .3997032   6.30  0.000   1.717976    3.32069
-------------+---------------------------------------------------------------
zeitmitmei~c |
 Spielklasse |   .272934  .1976238   1.38  0.173  -.1232779   .6691459
       _cons |  1.695982  .4458284   3.80  0.000   .8021497   2.589814
-------------+---------------------------------------------------------------
denterminv~e |
 Spielklasse |  .0667172  .1802497   0.37  0.713  -.2946616   .4280961
       _cons |  1.570129  .4066333   3.86  0.000   .7548783    2.38538
-------------------------------------------------------------------
```

Reasons for the Participation in the annual Test

.
.

. sum espflichtistkreisl ichnichtineinetieferespielklasse ichineinehherespielklasseaufstei ichdortzeigenkannwasichdraufha
> be unattraktivespielekreisl ichselbstherausfindenmchtewiegut regelkenntniskreisl ichdortdieanderenkollegenwieders

Variable	Obs	Mean	Std. Dev.	Min	Max
espflichti~l	54	4.203704	1.016461	1	5
ichnichtin~e	54	3.685185	1.489891	1	5
ichineineh~i	54	3.592593	1.523632	1	5
ichdortzei~e	54	3.592593	1.310603	1	5
unattrakti~l	54	3.092593	1.292482	1	5
ichselbsth~t	54	3.87037	1.099679	1	5
regelkennt~l	54	3.833333	1.023313	1	5
ichdortdie~s	54	3.148148	1.294508	1	5

.
.
.
.

. *Regression: Reasons for the Participation in the annual Test and Age*

.

.

. mvreg espflichtistkreisl ichnichtineinetieferespielklasse ichineinehherespielklasseaufstei ichdortzeigenkannwasichdrauf
> habe unattraktivespielekreisl ichselbstherausfindenmchtewiegut regelkenntniskreisl ichdortdieanderenkollegenwieders = A
> ltersklasse

Equation	Obs	Parms	RMSE	"R-sq"	F	P
espflichti~l	54	2	1.01389	0.0238	1.269211	0.2651
ichnichtin~e	54	2	1.463831	0.0529	2.90394	0.0943
ichineineh~i	54	2	1.374612	0.2014	13.11422	0.0007
ichdortzei~e	54	2	1.24714	0.1116	6.531207	0.0136
unattrakti~l	54	2	1.298881	0.0091	.4791075	0.4919
ichselbsth~t	54	2	1.106958	0.0058	.3053135	0.5829
regelkennt~l	54	2	1.010243	0.0438	2.38024	0.1289
ichdortdie~s	54	2	1.297632	0.0141	.7451369	0.3920

	Coef.	Std. Err.	t	P>|t|	[95% Conf. Interval]	
espflichti~l						
Altersklasse	-.1136364	.1008673	-1.13	0.265	-.3160414	.0887687
_cons	4.477273	.2792889	16.03	0.000	3.916839	5.037707
ichnichtin~e						
Altersklasse	-.2481672	.1456299	-1.70	0.094	-.5403949	.0440606
_cons	4.282625	.4032309	10.62	0.000	3.473483	5.091767
ichineineh~i						
Altersklasse	-.4952346	.1367539	-3.62	0.001	-.7696514	-.2208178
_cons	4.784824	.3786544	12.64	0.000	4.024998	5.54465
ichdortzei~e						
Altersklasse	-.3170821	.1240724	-2.56	0.014	-.5660515	-.0681127
_cons	4.355938	.3435408	12.68	0.000	3.666573	5.045303
unattrakti~l						
Altersklasse	-.0894428	.1292198	-0.69	0.492	-.3487413	.1698556
_cons	3.307918	.3577933	9.25	0.000	2.589953	4.025883
ichselbsth~t						
Altersklasse	-.0608504	.1101262	-0.55	0.583	-.2818349	.160134
_cons	4.016862	.3049257	13.17	0.000	3.404984	4.62874
regelkennt~l						
Altersklasse	.1550587	.1005045	1.54	0.129	-.0466184	.3567357
_cons	3.460044	.2782844	12.43	0.000	2.901625	4.018463
ichdortdie~s						
Altersklasse	-.111437	.1290955	-0.86	0.392	-.3704861	.1476122
_cons	3.416422	.3574493	9.56	0.000	2.699148	4.133697

Regression: Reasons for the Participation in the annual Test and Division

.
.

. mvreg espflichtistkreisl ichnichtineinetieferespielklasse ichineinehherespielklasseaufstei ichdortzeigenkannwasichdrauf
> habe unattraktivespielekreisl ichselbstherausfindenmchtewiegut regelkenntniskreisl ichdortdieanderenkollegenwieders = S
> pielklasse

```
Equation       Obs  Parms     RMSE     "R-sq"       F       P
-----------------------------------------------------------------------
espflichti~l    54    2   1.025326   0.0017   .0875434   0.7685
ichnichtin~e    54    2   1.467379   0.0483   2.638711   0.1103
ichineineh~i    54    2   1.533336   0.0063   .3312739   0.5674
ichdortzei~e    54    2   1.314398   0.0132   .6943871   0.4085
unattrakti~l    54    2   1.303004   0.0028   .1474624   0.7025
ichselbsth~t    54    2   1.103617   0.0118   .6224632   0.4337
regelkennt~l    54    2   1.033094   0.0000   .0011781   0.9728
ichdortdie~s    54    2   1.301457   0.0083   .435531    0.5122
```

```
----------------------------------------------------------------------------
          |    Coef.   Std. Err.     t    P>|t|    [95% Conf. Interval]
----------+-----------------------------------------------------------------
espflichti~l |
Spielklasse | -.0645432   .2181416   -0.30   0.769   -.5022763    .37319
     _cons |  4.341157   .485062     8.95   0.000    3.367809   5.314505
----------+-----------------------------------------------------------------
ichnichtin~e |
Spielklasse |  .5071249   .31219     1.62   0.110   -.1193302   1.13358
     _cons |  2.605197   .694189    3.75   0.000    1.212205   3.998189
----------+-----------------------------------------------------------------
ichineineh~i |
Spielklasse | -.1877619   .3262225   -0.58   0.567   -.8423753   .4668514
     _cons |  3.992456   .7253919   5.50   0.000    2.536851   5.448061
----------+-----------------------------------------------------------------
ichdortzei~e |
Spielklasse | -.233026    .2796427   -0.83   0.408   -.7941702   .3281182
     _cons |  4.088852   .6218166   6.58   0.000    2.841085   5.336618
----------+-----------------------------------------------------------------
unattrakti~l |
Spielklasse |  .1064543   .2772187    0.38   0.703   -.4498257   .6627344
     _cons |  2.865884   .6164265   4.65   0.000    1.628934   4.102835
----------+-----------------------------------------------------------------
ichselbsth~t |
Spielklasse | -.1852473   .2347983   -0.79   0.434   -.6564046    .28591
     _cons |  4.264878   .5221001   8.17   0.000    3.217208   5.312549
----------+-----------------------------------------------------------------
regelkennt~l |
Spielklasse |  .007544    .2197944    0.03   0.973   -.4335057   .4485937
     _cons |  3.817267   .4887371   7.81   0.000    2.836545   4.79799
----------+-----------------------------------------------------------------
ichdortdie~s |
Spielklasse | -.1827326   .2768895   -0.66   0.512   -.7383521   .3728869
     _cons |  3.537301   .6156945   5.75   0.000    2.30182    4.772782
----------------------------------------------------------------------------
```

Reasons for not participating in the annual Test

.

.

. sum ichankeinemderterminezeithatte ichangstvorzuvielenfehlernimrege weilichluferischnichtgutgenugbin ichsowiesonichtauf
> steigenkann weilmirjanichtspassiertwennichni weilichkeinelustdazuhatte weilichsowiesonichtineinetiefere

```
    Variable |   Obs     Mean   Std. Dev.   Min    Max
-------------+--------------------------------------------
  ichankeine~e |    36  2.833333  1.630074     1      5
  ichangstvo~e |    36  1.638889  .9900297     1      5
   weilichluf~n |    36  1.916667  1.105183     1      4
  ichsowieso~n |    36  2.361111  1.417297     1      5
   weilmirjan~i |    36  2.027778  1.230241     1      5
-------------+--------------------------------------------
  weilichkei~e |    36  1.722222    1.0586     1      5
  weilichsow~e |    36  2.277778  1.485378     1      5
```

.

.

.

. *Regression: Reasons for not participating in the annual Test and Age*

.

.

. mvreg ichankeinemderterminezeithatte ichangstvorzuvielenfehlernimrege weilichluferischnichtgutgenugbin ichsowiesonichta
> ufsteigenkann weilmirjanichtspassiertwennichni weilichkeinelustdazuhatte weilichsowiesonichtineinetiefere = Altersklass
> e

```
Equation       Obs  Parms    RMSE    "R-sq"      F       P
-----------------------------------------------------------------
ichankeine~e    36    2    1.603347  0.0602  2.176622  0.1493
ichangstvo~e    36    2    .9979745  0.0129  .4449502  0.5092
weilichluf~n    36    2    1.100289  0.0372  1.311992  0.2600
ichsowieso~n    36    2    1.40767   0.0417  1.480355  0.2321
weilmirjan~i    36    2    1.245718  0.0040  .1356916  0.7149
weilichkei~e    36    2    1.066332  0.0143  .4943189  0.4868
weilichsow~e    36    2    1.501378  0.0075  .2580239  0.6148
```

```
------------------------------------------------------------------
             |   Coef.  Std. Err.    t    P>|t|    [95% Conf. Interval]
-------------+----------------------------------------------------
ichankeine~e |
 Altersklasse | -.275188  .1865254  -1.48  0.149  -.6542531   .1038772
        _cons |  3.643609  .6107737   5.97  0.000   2.402368    4.88485
-------------+----------------------------------------------------
ichangstvo~e |
 Altersklasse | -.0774436  .1160994  -0.67  0.509  -.3133859   .1584987
        _cons |  1.866917  .3801651   4.91  0.000   1.094329   2.639506
-------------+----------------------------------------------------
weilichluf~n |
 Altersklasse |  .1466165  .1280022   1.15  0.260  -.1135152   .4067483
        _cons |  1.484962  .4191407   3.54  0.001   .6331661   2.336759
-------------+----------------------------------------------------
ichsowieso~n |
 Altersklasse |  .1992481  .1637613   1.22  0.232  -.1335549   .5320511
        _cons |  1.774436  .5362332   3.31  0.002   .6846792   2.864193
-------------+----------------------------------------------------
weilmirjan~i |
 Altersklasse | -.0533835  .1449206  -0.37  0.715  -.3478976   .2411307
        _cons |  2.184962  .4745397   4.60  0.000   1.220582   3.149343
-------------+----------------------------------------------------
weilichkei~e |
 Altersklasse |  .087218  .1240517   0.70  0.487  -.1648854   .3393214
        _cons |  1.465414  .4062049   3.61  0.001   .6399059   2.290921
-------------+----------------------------------------------------
weilichsow~e |
 Altersklasse |  .0887218  .1746628   0.51  0.615  -.2662357   .4436793
        _cons |  2.016541  .5719299   3.53  0.001   .8542399   3.178843
------------------------------------------------------------------
```

. *Regression: Reasons for not participating in the annual Test and Division*

.
.

. mvreg ichankeinemderterminezeithatte ichangstvorzuvielenfehlernimrege weilichluferischnichtgutgenugbin ichsowiesonichta
> ufsteigenkann weilmirjanichtspassiertwennichni weilichkeinelustdazuhatte weilichsowiesonichtineinetiefere = Spielklasse

Equation	Obs	Parms	RMSE	"R-sq"	F	P
ichankeine~e	36	2	1.582282	0.0847	3.146269	0.0851
ichangstvo~e	36	2	1.001867	0.0052	.1778418	0.6759
weilichluf~n	36	2	1.110516	0.0192	.6646467	0.4206
ichsowieso~n	36	2	1.433053	0.0069	.2346005	0.6312
weilmirjan~i	36	2	1.244322	0.0062	.2123438	0.6479
weilichkei~e	36	2	1.070445	0.0067	.2297029	0.6348
weilichsow~e	36	2	1.503852	0.0043	.1453766	0.7054

	Coef.	Std. Err.	t	P>|t|	[95% Conf. Interval]	
ichankeine~e						
Spielklasse	-.7622951	.4297592	-1.77	0.085	-1.635671	.1110808
_cons	4.442623	.9448189	4.70	0.000	2.52252	6.362726
ichangstvo~e						
Spielklasse	-.1147541	.2721142	-0.42	0.676	-.6677567	.4382485
_cons	1.881148	.5982389	3.14	0.003	.6653799	3.096915
weilichluf~n						
Spielklasse	.2459016	.3016241	0.82	0.421	-.3670722	.8588755
_cons	1.397541	.6631158	2.11	0.043	.0499275	2.745154
ichsowieso~n						
Spielklasse	.1885246	.3892275	0.48	0.631	-.6024809	.9795301
_cons	1.963115	.8557106	2.29	0.028	.2241016	3.702128
weilmirjan~i						
Spielklasse	-.1557377	.3379668	-0.46	0.648	-.8425689	.5310934
_cons	2.356557	.7430147	3.17	0.003	.8465699	3.866545
weilichkei~e						
Spielklasse	-.1393443	.2907407	-0.48	0.635	-.7302005	.451512
_cons	2.016393	.6391889	3.15	0.003	.7174052	3.315382
weilichsow~e						
Spielklasse	-.1557377	.4084572	-0.38	0.705	-.9858226	.6743472
_cons	2.606557	.8979867	2.90	0.006	.7816288	4.431486

Attitude towards Punishment / Fines

.
.

. sum einordnungsgeldfrdasunentschuldi diestrafevon5eurofrdasunentschul strafelehrabendhher strafelehrabendschrecktab ein
> ordnungsgeldfrdienichtteilnah ichfindeesgerechtdassichineineti diestrafenfrdasfernbleibenanlehr einordnungsgeldfrdiezuk
> urzfristi dasordnungsgeldfrdasunentschuldi

Variable	Obs	Mean	Std. Dev.	Min	Max
einordnun~di	50	1.22	.418452	1	2
diestrafev~l	53	1.245283	.4343722	1	2
strafelehr~r	47	1.723404	.4521508	1	2
strafelehr~b	49	1.693878	.4656573	1	2
einordnung~h	43	1.651163	.4822428	1	2
ichfindees~i	51	1.294118	.460179	1	2
diestrafen~r	35	1.2	.4058397	1	2
einordnun~ti	44	1.590909	.4973503	1	2
dasordnung~i	59	1.677966	.4712667	1	2

Regression: Attitude towards Punishment / Fines and Age

.
.
.

. mvreg einordnungsgeldfrdasunentschuldi diestrafevon5eurofrdasunentschul strafelehrabendhher strafelehrabendschrecktab e
> inordnungsgeldfrdienichtteilnah ichfindeesgerechtdassichineineti diestrafenfrdasfernbleibenanlehr einordnungsgeldfrdiez
> ukurzfristi dasordnungsgeldfrdasunentschuldi = Altersklasse

```
Equation      Obs Parms   RMSE    "R-sq"    F       P
-----------------------------------------------------------------
einordnun~di   18    2   .404921  0.1568  2.974697  0.1038
diestrafev~l   18    2   .4733138 0.1039  1.855072  0.1921
strafelehr~r   18    2   .4851697 0.0584  .9931034  0.3338
strafelehr~b   18    2   .5043104 0.0487  .8198582  0.3787
einordnung~h   18    2   .4376739 0.0148  .2410546  0.6301
ichfindees~i   18    2   .4128614 0.3182  7.466667  0.0148
diestrafen~r   18    2   .4276686 0.0594  1.009862  0.3299
einordnun~ti   18    2   .498374  0.0065  .1045752  0.7506
dasordnung~i   18    2   .5096472 0.0285  .4694444  0.5030
```

```
             | Coef.   Std. Err.   t    P>|t|   [95% Conf. Interval]
-------------+---------------------------------------------------------------
einordnun~di |
 Altersklasse| -.1125541 .0652589 -1.72  0.104  -.2508969  .0257886
        _cons|  1.541126 .2080795  7.41  0.000   1.100017  1.982234
-------------+---------------------------------------------------------------
diestrafev~l |
 Altersklasse| -.1038961 .0762814 -1.36  0.192  -.2656055  .0578133
        _cons|  1.627706 .2432249  6.69  0.000   1.112092  2.143319
-------------+---------------------------------------------------------------
strafelehr~r |
 Altersklasse| -.0779221 .0781922 -1.00  0.334  -.2436821  .0878379
        _cons|  1.887446 .2493174  7.57  0.000   1.358917  2.415975
-------------+---------------------------------------------------------------
strafelehr~b |
 Altersklasse|  .0735931 .081277   0.91  0.379  -.0987064  .2458926
        _cons|  1.402597 .2591534  5.41  0.000   .8532168  1.951978
-------------+---------------------------------------------------------------
einordnung~h |
 Altersklasse|  .034632  .0705375  0.49  0.630  -.1149009  .1841649
        _cons|  1.679654 .2249104  7.47  0.000   1.202865  2.156442
-------------+---------------------------------------------------------------
ichfindees~i |
 Altersklasse| -.1818182 .0665386 -2.73  0.015  -.3228738 -.0407626
        _cons|  1.848485 .2121599  8.71  0.000   1.398726  2.298244
-------------+---------------------------------------------------------------
diestrafen~r |
 Altersklasse|  .0692641 .068925   1.00  0.330  -.0768505  .2153786
        _cons|  1.025974 .2197689  4.67  0.000   .5600847  1.491863
-------------+---------------------------------------------------------------
einordnun~ti |
 Altersklasse| -.025974  .0803202 -0.32  0.751  -.1962453  .1442973
        _cons|  1.74026  .2561028  6.80  0.000   1.197346  2.283173
-------------+---------------------------------------------------------------
dasordnung~i |
 Altersklasse| -.0562771 .0821371 -0.69  0.503  -.2303999  .1178458
        _cons|  1.770563 .2618958  6.76  0.000   1.215368  2.325757
-------------+---------------------------------------------------------------
```

Regression: Attitude towards Punishment / Fines and Division

.
.

. mvreg einordnungsgeldfrdasunentschuldi diestrafevon5eurofrdasunentschul strafelehrabendhher strafelehrabendschrecktab e
> inordnungsgeldfrdienichtteilnah ichfindeesgerechtdassichineineti diestrafenfrdasfernbleibenanlehr einordnungsgeldfrdiez
> ukurzfristi dasordnungsgeldfrdasunentschuldi = Spielklasse

Equation	Obs	Parms	RMSE	"R-sq"	F	P
einordnun~di	18	2	.4308637	0.0453	.7585185	0.3967
diestrafev~l	18	2	.4987608	0.0050	.079602	0.7815
strafelehr~r	18	2	.4987608	0.0050	.079602	0.7815
strafelehr~b	18	2	.5073714	0.0372	.6175214	0.4435
einordnung~h	18	2	.4408026	0.0007	.0113234	0.9166
ichfindees~i	18	2	.4680378	0.1238	2.259887	0.1522
diestrafen~r	18	2	.4408026	0.0007	.0113234	0.9166
einordnun~ti	18	2	.4987608	0.0050	.079602	0.7815
dasordnung~i	18	2	.5170365	0.0001	.0020576	0.9644

	Coef.	Std. Err.	t	P>|t|	[95% Conf. Interval]	
einordnun~di						
Spielklasse	.1584158	.1818928	0.87	0.397	-.2271797	.5440114
_cons	.8613861	.4265764	2.02	0.061	-.0429155	1.765688
diestrafev~l						
Spielklasse	.0594059	.2105561	0.28	0.781	-.3869531	.505765
_cons	1.19802	.4937979	2.43	0.027	.151215	2.244825
strafelehr~r						
Spielklasse	-.0594059	.2105561	-0.28	0.781	-.505765	.3869531
_cons	1.80198	.4937979	3.65	0.002	.7551754	2.848785
strafelehr~b						
Spielklasse	.1683168	.2141912	0.79	0.443	-.2857482	.6223818
_cons	1.227723	.5023228	2.44	0.026	.162846	2.2926
einordnung~h						
Spielklasse	.019802	.1860886	0.11	0.917	-.3746882	.4142921
_cons	1.732673	.4364164	3.97	0.001	.8075118	2.657835
ichfindees~i						
Spielklasse	-.2970297	.1975862	-1.50	0.152	-.7158936	.1218342
_cons	2.009901	.4633806	4.34	0.001	1.027578	2.992224
diestrafen~r						
Spielklasse	-.019802	.1860886	-0.11	0.917	-.4142921	.3746882
_cons	1.267327	.4364164	2.90	0.010	.3421653	2.192488
einordnun~ti						
Spielklasse	-.0594059	.2105561	-0.28	0.781	-.505765	.3869531
_cons	1.80198	.4937979	3.65	0.002	.7551754	2.848785
dasordnung~i						
Spielklasse	-.009901	.2182714	-0.05	0.964	-.4726156	.4528136
_cons	1.633663	.5118917	3.19	0.006	.5485014	2.718825

Attitude towards Coaching

.
.
.
. sum ichglaubedassanderekollegenmirnt mirwreesunangenehmwennmichmitgli michwrdeesmotivierenwennmichmitg wennichvoneinemm
> itglieddeskreiss

```
    Variable |    Obs    Mean  Std. Dev.    Min    Max
-------------+--------------------------------------------
  ichglaubed~t |   60  3.616667  1.075011      1      5
  mirwreesun~i |   60  1.983333  1.096863      1      5
   michwrdees~g |   60  3.616667  1.236338      1      5
  wennichvon~s |   60      2.55  1.254483      1      5
```

.
.
.
.
. *Regression: Attitude towards Coaching and Age*

.
.
. mvreg ichglaubedassanderekollegenmirnt mirwreesunangenehmwennmichmitgli michwrdeesmotivierenwennmichmitg wennichvoneine
> mmitgliedeskreiss = Altersklasse

```
Equation      Obs  Parms    RMSE    "R-sq"        F        P
-----------------------------------------------------------------------
ichglaubed~t    60     2  1.001906  0.1461  9.924113  0.0026
mirwreesun~i    60     2  1.102764  0.0063  .3702026  0.5453
michwrdees~g    60     2  1.187996  0.0923  5.899323  0.0183
wennichvon~s    60     2  1.218668  0.0723  4.518877  0.0378
```

```
----------------------------------------------------------------------------
             |    Coef.  Std. Err.      t    P>|t|   [95% Conf. Interval]
-------------+--------------------------------------------------------------
ichglaubed~t |
  Altersklasse | -.2848995  .0904369  -3.15  0.003   -.4659287  -.1038703
        _cons |  4.347909  .2657267  16.36  0.000    3.815999   4.879818
-------------+--------------------------------------------------------------
mirwreesun~i |
  Altersklasse | -.0605649  .0995408  -0.61  0.545   -.2598176   .1386877
        _cons |  2.138783  .2924762   7.31  0.000    1.553328   2.724238
-------------+--------------------------------------------------------------
michwrdees~g |
  Altersklasse | -.2604563  .1072343  -2.43  0.018   -.4751091  -.0458035
        _cons |  4.285171  .3150816  13.60  0.000    3.654467   4.915875
-------------+--------------------------------------------------------------
wennichvon~s |
  Altersklasse | -.2338403  .1100029  -2.13  0.038    -.454035  -.0136456
        _cons |   3.15019  .3232164   9.75  0.000    2.503202   3.797178
----------------------------------------------------------------------------
```

Regression: Attitude towards Coaching and Division

.
.

. mvreg ichglaubedassanderekollegenmirnt mirwreesunangenehmwennmichmitgli michwrdeesmotivierenwennmichmitg wennichvoneine
> mmitglieddeskreiss = Spielklasse

```
Equation      Obs  Parms    RMSE    "R-sq"      F       P
-----------------------------------------------------------------
ichglaubed~t   60    2   1.059378  0.0453  2.754224  0.1024
mirwreesun~i   60    2   1.090708  0.0280  1.667759  0.2017
michwrdees~g   60    2   1.213978  0.0522  3.19339   0.0792
wennichvon~s   60    2   1.236401  0.0451  2.738397  0.1034
```

```
-------------------------------------------------------------------
            |   Coef.  Std. Err.    t   P>|t|   [95% Conf. Interval]
------------+------------------------------------------------------
ichglaubed~t |
Spielklasse | -.3615222  .2178388  -1.66  0.102  -.797574   .0745296
      _cons |  4.393939  .4879136   9.01  0.000   3.417274   5.370605
------------+------------------------------------------------------
mirwreesun~i |
Spielklasse | -.2896406  .2242811  -1.29  0.202  -.7385881   .1593069
      _cons |  2.606061  .502343    5.19  0.000   1.600512   3.611609
------------+------------------------------------------------------
michwrdees~g |
Spielklasse | -.4460888  .2496292  -1.79  0.079  -.9457758   .0535983
      _cons |  4.575758  .5591173   8.18  0.000   3.456563   5.694952
------------+------------------------------------------------------
wennichvon~s |
Spielklasse | -.4207188  .2542399  -1.65  0.103  -.9296353   .0881976
      _cons |  3.454545  .5694444   6.07  0.000   2.314679   4.594412
-------------------------------------------------------------------
```

Bribery and Game Manipulation

.
.

. list habensiebereitsimspielberichtein wieofthabensieimspielberichteine
eswurdemirschonmalgeldangebotend eswurdenmirmaxi
> malxyeurofrdiebev eswurdemirbeicircaxyspielengeldf

```
  +------------------------------------------+
  | habens~n  wieoft~e  eswurd~d  eswurd~v  eswurd~f |
  |------------------------------------------|
 1. |    2        .        2        .        . |
 2. |    2        .        2        .        . |
 3. |    2        .        2        .        . |
 4. |    2        .        1       100       1 |
 5. |    2        .        2        .        . |
  |------------------------------------------|
 6. |    2        .        2        .        . |
 7. |    1        .        2        .        . |
 8. |    2        .        2        .        . |
 9. |    2        .        2        .        . |
10. |    2        .        2        .        . |
  |------------------------------------------|
11. |    2        .        2        .        . |
12. |    2        .        2        .        . |
13. |    2        .        2        .        . |
14. |    1        .        2        .        . |
15. |    2        .        2        .        . |
  |------------------------------------------|
16. |    2        .        2        .        . |
17. |    2        .        2        .        . |
18. |    2        .        2        .        . |
19. |    1        2        1       30       10 |
20. |    1        1        1       50        1 |
  |------------------------------------------|
21. |    2        .        2        .        . |
22. |    2        .        2        .        . |
23. |    2        .        1       200       . |
24. |    2        .        2        .        . |
25. |    2        .        2        .        . |
  |------------------------------------------|
26. |    2        .        2        .        . |
27. |    2        .        2        .        . |
28. |    2        .        2        .        . |
29. |    2        .        2        .        . |
30. |    2        .        1        .        . |
  |------------------------------------------|
31. |    2        .        1       100       . |
32. |    2        .        2        .        . |
33. |    1        1        2        .        . |
34. |    2        .        2        .        . |
35. |    2        .        2        .        . |
  |------------------------------------------|
36. |    2        .        2        .        . |
37. |    1        2        1       300       3 |
38. |    2        .        2        .        . |
39. |    2        .        2        .        . |
40. |    2        .        2        .        . |
  |------------------------------------------|
41. |    2        .        2        .        . |
42. |    2        .        2        .        . |
43. |    2        .        2        .        . |
44. |    2        .        2        .        . |
45. |    2        .        2        .        . |
  |------------------------------------------|
46. |    2        .        2        .        . |
47. |    2        .        2        .        . |
48. |    2        .        2        .        . |
49. |    2        .        2        .        . |
50. |    2        .        2        .        . |
  |------------------------------------------|
51. |    2        .        2        .        . |
52. |    2        .        2        .        . |
53. |    2        .        2        .        . |
54. |    2        .        1        .        1 |
55. |    2        .        2        .        . |
  |------------------------------------------|
56. |    2        .        2        .        . |
57. |    2        .        .        .        . |
58. |    2        .        1       150       2 |
59. |    2        .        2        .        . |
60. |    2        .        2        .        . |
  +------------------------------------------+
```

.
.
.

. *Closing the Log-File*

.
. log close

List of Abbreviations

PAT	Principal-Agent Theory
PR	Public Relations
U.S.A	United States of America
KSA	Kreis-Schiedsrichterausschuss
KSO	Kreis-Schiedsrichterobmann
K34	Kreis 34 (Kreis Guetersloh)
FLVW	Fußball- und Leichtathletik-Verband Westfalen
FVN	Fußball-Verband Niederrhein
FVM	Fußball-Verband Mittelrhein
WFLV	Westdeutscher Fußball- und Leichtathletikverband
DFB	Deutscher Fußball-Bund
EUR	Euro
NRW	North Rhine-Westfalia
TV	Television

List of Figures